COLLABORATIVE INTERVENTION:
HOW TO IDENTIFY, ASSESS, AND INTERVENE IN TROUBLED TECHNOLOGY AND TRANSFORMATION PROJECTS

ROB PRINZO

ISBN: 0983033501
ISBN-13: 978-0-9830335-0-9

DEDICATION

For C. K. & T.

COLLABORATIVE INTERVENTION

CONTENTS

Introduction

Throughout my career as an enterprise technology and transformation consultant, I have found that most projects fail due to human factors early in the project life cycle. Using these lessons learned as a foundation, I developed a Three-Step Project Quality Assurance methodology known as Collaborative Intervention®. Collaborative Intervention enables organizations to periodically stop and address project failure before it occurs.

Three years ago, to illustrate the concepts of Collaborative Intervention, I wrote *No Wishing Required: The Business Case for Project Assurance.* Since writing *No Wishing Required,* I have continued to work with organizations as an advisor and project manager on complex, large-scale, enterprise projects. Through these engagements, I validated the need to educate organizations on the concepts of Collaborative Intervention. I also learned that although the concepts of Collaborative Intervention were originally intended for project managers, project team members and executives benefited just as much, if not more, from these concepts, since many of them had not previously been exposed to a formal methodology for the projects they were participating in.

For this reason, I decided to publish a more comprehensive book on the Collaborative Intervention methodology. While *No Wishing Required* is written as a novel, this book serves as a methodology guide. However, because the story in *No Wishing Required* provides relatable examples of the application of the Collaborate Intervention methodology, I have incorporated one of the case studies from *No Wishing* into this book.

Collaborative Intervention is a registered trademark of The Prinzo Group.

Section 1—An Introduction to Collaborative Intervention

The Light at the End of the Tunnel

You are on a software implementation project and begin to ask yourself, *"How could this be happening?"* The last project was so much better. Sure, there were issues, but you were able to transition to the new system and provide the users with the support they needed. However, this new project is a disaster. Nothing seems to be going right and nobody knows what to do about it. Development is behind, top management is not engaged and the users are fighting the implementation team. You are starting to get the feeling that the light at the end of the tunnel is actually an oncoming train.

Have you ever been in this situation? If so, it may be why you're reading this book. I know I've been in

4

situations like this—and more than once. On some occasions the situation was less dramatic. But occasionally it was arguably worse. There is a silver lining, however, in that these experiences occurred early enough in my career that I've been able to carry forward the lessons I learned and embed them within the project assurance practices that this book is about. No one wins all the time, and if you are resourceful and tenacious, you can learn more from failure than from success. Now don't get me wrong; as a consultant I've been involved in many highly successful projects. But the lessons I learned the hard way are the ones that formed a firm foundation for future success.

Over the years, I have been involved in projects of all shapes and sizes, ranging from implementing add-on modules to Enterprise Resource Planning Systems (ERP) to organization-wide transformation projects. I have sat on all sides of the desk: consultant (developer, trainer, project manager, executive partner); customer (technology director); and software vendor (on-site consultant). My goal in this book is to give you the insights you need to learn from these experiences and share the tools I've developed to help you navigate the complexities of enterprise project implementations.

Over the last twenty-five years, advances in technology have provided organizations with software to automate their business functions:

finance, human resources, customer relationship management, supply chain management, shop floor control, etc. The purpose of these systems is to make the interaction between internal business processes, customers, and suppliers a seamless transaction. However, the selection and implementation of these systems is anything but seamless. In fact, the selection and implementation of these systems is downright complicated. If you work in the business world, you have likely heard or experienced horror stories with enterprise software implementations that range from daily headaches to loss of business. At the end of the day, enterprise technology has changed dramatically during this time, *but human behavior has not.*

In fact, the horror stories continue. Consider the facts that industry experts published over the last several years:

A 2008 publication from Accenture cites that:
- IT projects come in at a success rate of only 29 percent.
- Average cost overrun is 56 percent.
- The average schedule delay is 84 percent beyond plan. [1]

Simply translated, this means that nearly 70 percent of implementations will fail, cost more than 50 percent over budget, and take nearly twice as long as planned.

A 2010 KPMG survey of project management practices in New Zealand survey shows that:

- 70 percent of organizations have suffered at least one project failure in the prior twelve months.
- 50 percent of respondents also indicated that their project failed to consistently achieve what they set out to achieve.[2]

A 2012 study by McKinsey in collaboration with the University of Oxford suggests:

- Half of all large IT projects with initial costs greater than $15 million massively exceed their budgets.
- On average, large IT projects run 45 percent over budget and 7 percent over time, while delivering 56 percent less value than predicted.[3]

The extreme complexity and poor success rate of software implementations continue to baffle many executives. Given that there are accredited bodies of knowledge surrounding software implementations, certifications for project management professionals, a growing field of highly skilled practitioners, endless tools and methodologies, and countless studies on what makes projects successful—why do projects still fail? The failures can range from project cost overruns, missed expectations, and disgruntled users, to "train wrecks"—which are wastelands of time and money in the form of software that is never implemented or projects that are simply canceled.

With so many organizations making huge investments of time and money while continuing to experience less than successful outcomes with these large-scale projects, I began to ask myself, *what if there was a way to assure project success—or at minimum, to increase the odds of success?*

To address this question, I investigated the history of software implementations and why projects fail. Combining my research with personal experience, I realized that failure is avoidable. Armed with this certainty, I developed a repeatable process for managing projects to succeed by addressing failure before it occurs.

The Evolution of Enterprise Business Applications—*and Why It Matters*

There are lessons to be learned from history in understanding why projects fail. To begin with, let's cruise through the evolution of enterprise business systems over the last half-century.

Mainframes and Minis—Automating Manual Processes

In the early days of software implementation or system development, the automation of manual, repetitive tasks or the transfer of paper-based processes online were business process improvements in and of themselves. Organizations did not spend great lengths of time analyzing their business processes as part of a system

9

implementation. The focus was purely on *system implementation*, a term we still use today.

During the early days of system implementations, software was centralized on large mainframe systems, data was stored in flat file structures, and data was updated in "batches," typically overnight. For these early adopter organizations, implementing technology meant changing the way business was done in order to accommodate the system's functionality.

At first, companies developed their own business systems in-house until industry pioneers such as Management Science America (MSA), McCormack & Dodge (M&D), and Teserac developed the first packaged software applications to automate basic business functions such as general ledger accounting and payroll. These systems were often implemented by the consulting arm of a "Big 8" (at the time) accounting firm or system integrators such as IBM or EDS.

Enterprise Resource Planning (ERP) Systems and Client/Server—*Improving Business Processes*

In the 1990s, the technology promise was *"improving business processes"* and to achieve it, companies had to go through a substantial technology shift. This shift consisted of moving away from the centralized mainframe systems to "client/server" technologies where applications were loaded on individual user workstations (the client) and the data was maintained and stored in relational databases (the server). Major software providers began developing their mainframe products for the client/server environment and new players emerged.

The whole paradigm shift was accelerated by the Y2K bug. "The practice of representing the year with two digits becomes problematic with logical error(s) arising upon 'rollover' from x99 to x00. This has caused some date-related processing to operate incorrectly on and after January 1, 2000 and on other critical dates that were billed 'event horizons.' Without corrective action, it was suggested that long-working systems would break down when the '...97, 98, 99, 00...' ascending numbering assumption suddenly became invalid. Companies and organizations worldwide checked, fixed, and upgraded their computer systems..."[4]

As companies scrambled to implement new systems with the dual hopes of making a technology leap and avoiding the Y2K bug, systems were replaced and Y2K avoided. But there was collateral damage in terms of systems that did not meet business requirements. Most organizations underestimated the ongoing commitment required to implement, integrate, and optimize their enterprise applications, resulting in failure to realize the expected benefits. This failure, in turn, led to quick-fix solutions that added to an organization's frustration with its investments in enterprise applications.

Enterprise application implementation frustration extended to some of the world's best-run companies. According to the Hackett Group's *Profile of World Class Finance*, even world-class organizations spent "too much time and money on routine transaction processing activity and wrestling with partially implemented systems that have failed to deliver the return on investment."[5]

The failure of many enterprise application initiatives to deliver results can be traced back to these factors:

- Rushed implementations of the enterprise application as a Year 2000 remedy
- Underestimation of the complexity of the system implementation and the impact that a large-scale enterprise application has on the organization
- Immature product releases that were rushed to market
- Failure of product vendors to deliver applications that met expectations set during the sales process
- Amount of skilled integration resources available to meet customer demand.

The Y2K Hangover/ERP 2.0—*the Wild, Wild Web*

As struggling implementations moved into the maintenance and support phase, the dot-com technology bubble burst and organizations scaled back their investments in enterprise applications. Enterprise software applications became viewed as transactional systems. Little or no thought was given to the long-term strategy beyond implementation, and organizations believed that their investments in enterprise applications would decrease. As the organization adjusted to life with its new applications, the implementation cost myth disintegrated—it was discovered that over a five-year period, acquisition and implementation costs constituted only 30 percent of the total cost of ownership of enterprise applications.[6]

One of the main challenges to the implementation cost myth that organizations encountered after initial implementation was the upgrade. As enterprise application vendors caught up to market demand, technology, and the Internet, organizations were faced with upgrading both their applications and supporting technology platforms. For some early adopters, upgrading to the web platform would constitute their second or third upgrade in five years. The latest upgrades to the web or Internet platform would provide much of the anticipated benefits to streamline business processes through self-service and integration, but organizations were still struggling with existing business requirements including unimplemented modules and the inability to access key decision-making information.

Between 2003 and 2005, most organizations stabilized their business in the aftermath of the 2001 recession. Enterprise applications themselves had become more stabilized. Software vendors were able to catch up with software defects and provide more reliable applications. The Gartner Group predicted that these business applications would contribute more to the business value than any other IT investments in more than 90 percent of organizations through 2007.[7]

Organizations began to realize that more structure was required for the effective management of technology. This realization led to the creation of project governance in the form of ERP steering committees composed of executives from the business functions and IT, the creation of Project Management Offices, and a surge in the number of project managers pursuing PMP© certifications.

PMP is a registered mark of the Project Management Institute, Inc.

The Global Recession—*Accelerated Change*

Beginning in 2008, the economic downturn and great recession had a significant impact on enterprise system implementations and the following trends emerged:

- Acceleration of consolidated and shared services. The move to consolidated and shared services was overdue and is now being driven by cost savings through position reductions. Organizational opponents of these initiatives are left defenseless, as their disparate units can no longer support the cost of doing things themselves.

- Outsourcing is continuing and growing. Buying more services at lower rates is compelling. Once again, internal opponents are left defenseless as they can no longer compete with cheap labor.

- Software as a Service (SaaS) has become a more attractive option. Proven business vendors and feature-rich software from companies such as Salesforce.com and Workday are driving traditional vendors to offer their products as a service.

- The need to upgrade. As the economy recovered, spending on enterprise applications and IT was deferred until confidence improved. Technology moves forward and drives change in the form of upgrades. Most organizations halted spending on enterprise business applications, because for the most part, they could get by with what is in place.

The History Lesson

The technology waves and economic cycles of the last few decades have shown us that:

- Business systems have evolved from "having a system" to complex and integrated systems that may or may not be housed within organizations

- Technology moves forward and organizations will continue to invest in both upgrades and new technologies

- Enterprise technology projects have become increasingly more complicated as organizations internally are integrating systems that cross traditional business functions and externally have more vendor partners involved in technology projects

- Despite the cumulative expertise gained from implementing enterprise systems, projects still have a 70 percent rate of failure.

The combination of technology and market influences creates inflection points for technology projects and implementations. The inflection point occurs when organizations that are financially ready to reinvest in enterprise systems, realize that upgrading the application will cost as much as implementing the software in the first place, and wonder whether there are better options on the market to meet their needs.

The inflection point raises these questions:

- Should we upgrade or find a new system?
- Is this a business we want to be in or should we; outsource the business process, outsource the infrastructure, or evaluate software as a service?
- Do we need to change how we do business and consider a business transformation project by evaluating systems as part of a business process?

Why Projects Fail

You would think that, over the years, project management would have evolved along with the technology that is being implemented. In truth, the high rate of project failure in today's organizations is proof that project implementation methodologies have not kept pace.

So, why do projects fail?

1. Lack of top management commitment

2. Unrealistic expectations

3. Poor definition of requirements

4. Improper package selection

5. Gaps between software and business requirements

6. Inadequate resources

7. Underestimating time and cost

8. Poor project management/lack of methodology

9. Underestimating the impact of change

10. Lack of training/education

Look closely—you may be surprised to see that a common denominator is not technology, *but people*.

People's decisions, expectations, and actions are the key components in project success—and failure. When I worked on PeopleSoft implementations, I was often quoted as saying, "If you took the People out of a PeopleSoft project, it would be easy to implement." Why? Because for the most part, software is coded to perform a function, but people and/or the project team members are required to develop the plan, evaluate systems and services, manage the implementation, design and configure the application, test the system, train the users, and communicate the change to the organization.

At the same time consider the evolution of project management methodologies.

Standard Methodology for Software Implementation

Today's software implementation methodology is adopted from the waterfall model used in the manufacturing and construction industries. The waterfall model is a sequential implementation process where each phase follows a previous phase flowing steadily downward like a waterfall.

Waterfall methodology

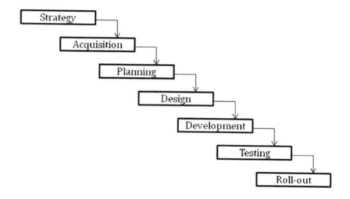

Since no formal methodology was available at the time of the first enterprise system implementations, the waterfall model has become the de facto methodology used by companies and systems integrators. Over the years, it has evolved to account for ongoing project activities such as project management and change management.

The waterfall methodology is the most structured of the methods, stepping through requirements, analysis, design, coding, and testing in a strict, pre-planned, "all at once" sequence. Progress is often measured in terms of deliverable artifacts:

requirement specifications, design documents, test plans, code reviews, and the like.

A common criticism of the waterfall model is its inflexible division of a project into separate stages, in which commitments are made early on, making it difficult to react to changes in requirements as the project executes. This means that the waterfall model is likely to be unsuitable if requirements are not well understood or defined, or are changed in the course of the project.[8]

Inflexible, archaic project management methodologies can result in significant cost overruns as well as failure to meet the fundamental business requirements of the software implementation over the course of the project. After the purchase, the most significant cost occurs during the development phase. If, during the strategy phase, there are gaps in the business requirements and the implementation plan, it could spell disaster for the implementation itself.

To head off disaster before it occurs, I decided to map the reasons that projects fail to the timed phases of a software implementation. What I found was intriguing: Although failure points are present throughout the project life cycle, *most, if not all, can occur before the project technically begins.*

Why Projects Fail

Reasons Projects Fail	Strategy	Acquisition	Planning	Design	Development	Testing	Roll-out
1. Lack of Top Management Commitment	X	X	X	X	X	X	X
2. Unrealistic Expectations	X	X	X	X	X	X	
3. Poor Requirements Definition	X	X		X			
4. Improper Package Selection		X					
5. Gaps between software and business requirements		X		X			
6. Inadequate Resources			X	X	X	X	
7. Underestimating Time and Costs			X	X	X		
8. Poor Project Management / Lack of Methodology			X	X	X	X	
9. Underestimating the Impact of Change			X		X		X
10. Lack of Training / Education			X		X	X	X

Reliance on Tools and Templates

The top reasons that projects fail really haven't changed. The reality is that most project teams are aware of why projects fail, but don't know how to address the reasons. Instead, most project managers look to "tools" or "templates" to guide them. I've seen countless documents and spreadsheets for requirements gathering and mapping, tracking users' skills and training needs, and even stakeholder analysis and involvement. The problem is not the lack of tools; it's a lack of understanding and review of the content of those tools. Yes, tools and templates provide a structure for content, but the content itself is gathered and evaluated by the project team.

In addition to tools and templates, people today expect software to solve problems for them. In fact, I hesitate to use the term "collaborative" intervention because "collaborative" is the connotation today for collaborative software. Collaborative software is both a blessing and a curse. It is a blessing in terms of its ability to share project documents, collect online feedback, and provide project workspaces. It is a curse in that it doesn't address the reasons projects fail or create the environment for their resolution. If a project is off track and needs an intervention, that intervention needs to happen in person. Why? Some of the issues that may be discussed will be too sensitive for an impersonal online discussion. Chat sessions are not the best way to resolve complex business problems. There is a need for personal interaction: the need to observe facial expressions, have eye contact, and observe body language and voice tone in order to get full information from all dimensions.

Ensuring project success requires doing what is obvious but not easy. You simply can't wish away problems; you need to confront and resolve them before they become insurmountable.

I can't count the number of times that project team members or project managers have brought issues to my attention that require a conversation with another team member. My first question is always, "Have you talked with so-and-so?" and nine times out of ten, the answer is, "No, but we exchanged some emails." After evaluating the email chain, the culprits are usually both miscommunication and misunderstanding. Project team members can hide behind e-mails and other collaborative software packages to avoid the issue. No matter how much technology exists to manage projects with online communication packages, often times complex project issues need to be resolved with a face-to-face discussion.

I was involved in a situation where senior executives responsible for different business functions (IT, HR, and Finance) were joined in a system implementation project. The three executives were each in a silo within their own organizations and did not meet or talk with one another. In fact, they each thought the other one was "out to get me" and had different perceptions of the other person's intentions. However, these perceptions were incorrect. As it turned out, they were actually on the same page about several pressing project issues. How did I know this? I talked to each one of them individually and asked them what their intentions were. As it turns out, they were in alignment. At the end of my visit, I had a joint meeting with all three of them and we resolved the issues. No technology required.

Reliance on Certifications

In addition to the reliance on tools, templates, and collaborative software, there has been a movement to require project managers to complete the PMP certification. Project Management Professional

(PMP) is a credential offered by the Project Management Institute (PMI). As of mid-2009, there were over 350,000 PMP-certified individuals worldwide. The credential is obtained by documenting three or five years' work experience in project management, completing thirty-five hours of project management–related training, and scoring a certain percentage of questions on a written, multiple-choice examination.[10]

For a large, complex project, a PMP certification is just the price of admission, since it provides a common language and methodology for project management. However, few studies correlate the success rates of projects to whether the project manager is PMP-certified. Experience implementing projects of similar scope and nature can be more important than having a PMP, since a PMP provides the framework for *managing* large-scale projects, not knowledge about the specifics regarding system implementations. Organizations that choose "generic" project managers with PMP certifications, but who lack domain knowledge, will surely struggle with elusive project success.

To me, project management experience and domain knowledge about the type of software you are implementing is 50 percent of success. The other 50 percent lies in understanding the organization and knowing how to navigate the organizational structure to advance project goals. In addition, that second 50 percent success factor relies heavily on communication skills and business acumen— something not easily obtained through a PMP certification.

Lack of Project Assurance Methodologies

Over the last several years, there has been an increasing adoption of Independent Verification and Validation (IV&V) for large-scale IT projects, especially in the government space. IV&V is defined as follows:

"Verification and validation is the process conducted by a third party that checks that a product, service, or system meets specifications and that it fulfills its intended purpose. These are critical components of a quality management system such as ISO 9000.

IV&V is comprised of three components:

- Independent ensures the validation is performed by a disinterested or impartial third party.

- Verification is a quality control process that is used to evaluate whether or not a product, service, or system complies with regulations, specifications, or conditions imposed at the start of a development phase. Verification can be in development, scale-up, or production. This is often an internal process.

- Validation is the quality assurance process of establishing evidence that provides a high degree of assurance that a product, service, or system accomplishes its intended requirements. This often involves acceptance of fitness for purpose with end users and other product stakeholders."[10]

Just like project management, the IV&V processes have been adopted from other industries such as construction, manufacturing, food and drug, and engineering, to name a few. The concepts of verification, *"Are we building the right thing?"* and validation, *"Are we building it right?"* were first introduced in technology for custom software development and the application of quality assurance programs such as ISO and CMMI. These process-oriented development projects rely heavily on hands-on software testing to determine whether the product built does indeed meet the business requirements. The problem with this approach when implementing packaged software is that the failure points occur long before testing. Certainly, IV&V can tactically help reduce software defects to improve user acceptance, but it does not test and validate the strategic direction of the project.

In addition, applying standard IV&V concepts to project management falls short in the following areas:

- There is no common language or methodology for IV&V software implementation projects. Most IV&V projects are project audits that address obvious gaps in deliverables.

- Utilizing a general project management point of view can mean missing details associated with packaged software implementation— such as software interdependences and joint organizational responsibilities.

- The concepts address tactical project issues and do not offer strategic solutions to project issues.

The High Cost of Failure

As mentioned in the previous section, project failure can happen early, producing a ripple effect on your project. In planning your project, you have calculated your project budget, resource/staffing needs, and your projected ROI. However, if there is a gap in your requirements that causes a delay during the acquisition phase of the project, or, worse yet, you leave out key requirements from the strategy phase because of a rushed assessment, the resulting impact will be seen downstream—causing the extension of subsequent project phases. The ripple effect of missing project gaps early during the project will not only create vulnerability and weakness in the project plan integrity, it affects the timeline, the overall project cost, realized benefits/ROI calculations, and the project team's credibility.

For example, project delay cost can be measured as follows:

Internal and external resources cost—a three-month project delay resulting in the extension of two internal resources at $120,000 a year, plus the extension of three consultants at $175 per hour, results in over $350,000 in extra project costs.

Delayed operational improvements and realization of operational improvements—a three-month project delay with additional resource cost will lower the projected return on investment (ROI) by delaying the realization of the system benefits in the form of cost saving and streamlined business processes.

Loss of confidence in the project team itself—missed project deadlines result in lower project team morale and organizational skepticism about the viability of the current and future projects.

The Business Case for a Better Way

History is repeating itself: The impact of the global recession on technology spending is creating the latest inflection point for enterprise systems. The inflection point occurs when organizations realize that upgrading the application will cost as much as the original implementation. As the economy improved, organizations began enterprise system projects in the form of business process transformation projects, and new system implementations or upgrades.

But how can we improve the odds for implementation success? As you can see from our analysis of project failure, projects will continue to fail due to human factors, with the most common and fatal failure points occurring early in the project—making the cost of failure exponential.

Inherent in the analysis of failure is the software implementation methodology itself (the waterfall methodology). As a stand-alone, legacy project management methodology, it does not have the checks and balances required to ensure success during the strategy, acquisition, and planning stages. It does not provide the mechanisms for project interventions.

By combining the lessons learned with the analysis of why projects fail, the alarming fact is that after all these years, while the level of expertise in enterprise system implementations has increased, the success rate has not. Future failures are imminent because many organizations lack the ability, tools, and knowledge to ensure that projects are delivered on time, on-budget, and with user acceptance, or, to put it another way, *organizations lack project assurance.*

The Need for Project Assurance

How can any organization that is considering implementing a large-scale enterprise system disregard the need for project assurance? Project assurance is about making sure that projects are delivered on time, on-budget, and with client acceptance. Having project assurance as part of a large-scale system implementation or transformation project helps to:

- Control/reduce project costs

- Ensure milestones are met

- Minimize surprises

- Provide objective analysis

- Provide peace of mind and trust among executives and project team members.

If you don't have a genie handy, project assurance is the closest thing to an insurance policy for enterprise application software implementations that you can get.

What is Collaborative Intervention?

How do you know if failure lies ahead? Often you don't. But if you stand back and look at the situation as if you were watching a movie, you may see the signs of impending disaster. Picture this scene: a train speeding down the track; a hurried driver in a car trying to make it across the tracks as the train rounds the curve; the conductor not paying attention; the crossing bars going down; the red lights flashing; the bells ringing. Watching the movie, how can you miss what is about to happen?

Picturing the project as a movie works if you can stand back from the project, but the truth is that most people on the project team can't see the train wreck that is about to occur, or, if they do see it, they don't know how to stop it. That is why Collaborative Intervention is so innovative: It is a process to avert disaster by identifying the warning signs and taking preventative action.

Collaborative Intervention is a project assurance methodology designed to align project expectations, resources, and scope with the goal of increasing the project's probability of success. Collaborative Intervention is different from other project assurance methodologies in that it addresses key project failure points before they occur. How? By creating a collaborative environment composed of key project stakeholders to identify and resolve project issues and avert roadblocks as they arise.

Most project teams may not encounter one large disaster but rather a series of small disasters that can lead up to larger failure. Like the train wreck scenario above, different parts of the project team may be unaware that they are on a collision course. Individual events, such as the driver running late or the conductor being distracted, may be caused by events that took place earlier. The same is true for project failure. For example, not conducting a needs assessment, missing requirements, choosing the wrong software or implementation partner, or underestimating the impact of change can all be identified early on and corrected to lessen the downstream impact.

Collaborative Intervention is an ongoing process that evaluates warning signs at the points at which they are likely to begin to occur in the project. Collaborative Intervention allows project managers and executives to take action, to monitor the situation to make sure that the issues are resolved, and, if they are not, to adjust accordingly. By establishing a framework of Collaborative Intervention, organizations can ensure that project failure points are averted before they occur and avert the disastrous train wreck from ever materializing.

The Collaborative Intervention methodology is based on the following best practices:

1. Identify the real issues. At the leadership level, you need to develop an executive dialogue that allows business and organizational issues to be identified and analyzed with clarity and without emotion. Continue this dialogue throughout the implementation process. Remove organizational barriers both within the organization and with third-party vendors. All parties should be aligned with the common goal of project success.

2. Set realistic time frames. Don't rely on the existing schedule. Many organizations will set overly optimistic go-live dates in spite of the realities and limitations of the actual project.

For example, the design phase extends beyond the current estimates... but the overall project timeline does not change. You must monitor project progress throughout the implementation and start discussions regarding key project dates early in the project's life cycle to avoid downstream impacts.

3. Align the work streams. You need to identify, align, and continuously monitor work streams to ensure smooth progress throughout the organization. Understand dependencies between work streams during project plan development to ensure proper resource allocations and project time frames. Continue to monitor the interdependencies throughout the project.

4. Look beyond the indicators. Contrary to popular opinion, green may actually be red. Realistic monitoring and analysis of progress of the implementation can show that even though all project management indicators are green, warning signs indicate endangered components. If indicators are only addressing past phases, but not addressing the readiness for upcoming project tasks and activities, they are definitely trailing indicators and not trustworthy predictions of the future.

5. Manage the expectations. To maintain

control of the project it is critical to manage the confluence of overly optimistic go-live dates against outside influences and interdependencies, such as available resources and realistic expectations. Set realistic expectations up front and keep expectations current in the mind of project team members so that they don't lose sight of the forest while maneuvering around a tree.

6. Seek objectivity. Assessments conducted by an outside expert add both value to the project implementation and protection against the high cost of failure. Expertise delivers the know-how and the objective oversight needed to overcome organizational roadblocks. It also provides you with peace of mind. Assessments should be conducted by an executive project manager or software implementation expert who has managed enough projects successfully to know how to recognize subtle indicators, intervene to accommodate the situation, and adjust expectations accordingly.

The Collaborative Intervention Process

Collaborative Intervention is composed of three steps: Identify, Assess, and Intervene.

Collaborative Intervention

1. **Identify**—The first step of the Collaborative Intervention process is to identify where the project is in the implementation life cycle, so that you understand **when** to intervene. Once determined, you can know what to look for and what the likely issues may be.

2. **Assess**—The second step of the Collaborative Intervention process is to assess. The assessment is a top-to-bottom evaluation of **what** to look for during the project to help you align project expectations, resources, and scope with the goal of increasing the project's probability of success.

3. **Intervene**—The final stage of the Collaborative Intervention process is to intervene. The Collaborative Intervention process outlines **how** to intervene by presenting the findings of the assessment and working with the project team to develop an implementation plan to address the findings.

At the end of the day, Collaborative Intervention gives you the *when, what, and how* answers you need to assure project success. It helps you to identify and resolve the strategic, tactical, and intangible issues before they become insurmountable. Collaborative Intervention gives you the tools and techniques you need to investigate and defuse volatile situations within the organization and the project team.

And best of all, Collaborative Intervention gives you (and everyone else involved) peace of mind that the project is on the right track.

How to Become an Interventionist

Identify

Your first step in the Collaborative Intervention process is to identify where the project is in the implementation lifecycle in order to know when to intervene. That knowledge will help you to understand what to look for and what the likely issues may be at that particular stage of the implementation.

Collaborative Intervention

Collaborative Intervention addresses project failure points before they occur. If we take the top reasons projects fail and overlay them across the project implementation lifecycle, what emerges is that while the reasons for project failure are present throughout the implementation, all have potentially occurred at least once by the third stage of the project: planning.

If you fail to address these potential failure issues early on, they will linger and grow malignantly throughout the project, causing further issues downstream. Based upon when failure is likely to occur within the traditional stages of the project life cycle, I have identified six key points in time where an assessment and intervention will have the greatest impact.

Reasons Projects Fail	Strategy	Acquisition	Planning	Design	Development	Testing	Roll-out
1. Lack of Top Management Commitment	X	X	X	X	X	X	X
2. Unrealistic Expectations	X	X	X	X	X	X	
3. Poor Requirements Definition	X	X		X			
4. Improper Package Selection		X					
5. Gaps between software and business requirements		X		X			
6. Inadequate Resources			X	X	X	X	
7. Underestimating Time and Costs			X	X	X		
8. Poor Project Management / Lack of Methodology			X	X	X	X	
9. Underestimating the Impact of Change			X		X		X
10. Lack of Training / Education			X		X	X	X

I often refer to conducting the assessments at these critical stages in the system implementation life cycle as "sampling the soup. " Just as a master chef samples the soup and adjusts the flavors throughout the cooking process, a project executive can intervene at these critical stages in a project's life cycle to ensure that the project is compliant with best practices, project gaps are being addressed, and expectations are being properly managed.

The six critical stages to intervene in a project are as follows:

1. During the strategy phase, before the business case is presented for approval and funding. The purpose of the first assessment is to address top management's commitment to the project, expectations, and requirements definition.

2. During the acquisition phase, toward the end of the vendor selection process, before vendors are finalized and negotiations begin. The purpose of the second assessment is to address the software and services selection and gaps between the proposed software and/or services and the business requirements.

3. Toward the end of the planning phase, after the initial drafts of the Project Charter, Detailed Project Plan, and Change Management Plans have been developed. The purpose of the third assessment is to

ensure that there is a strong project management methodology in place, that the project has adequate resources, and that the timeline and scope are realistic.

4. Toward the end of the design phase, after the initial drafts of the System Design Documentation have been developed. The purpose of the fourth assessment is to ensure that there are minimal gaps between the software and the business requirements, that the organization understands the impact of the change, and that the project has adequate resources allocated.

5. The fifth assessment should be conducted toward the end of the development phase. The purpose is to ensure that the project management methodology for testing is in place, that the impact of organizational change is being addressed, and that the proposed education and training plans will meet user requirements.

6. The final assessment should be conducted toward the end of the testing and training phase. The purpose of the sixth assessment is to ensure that top management is committed to the project for the system cutover and the next phases of the project,

that there are adequate resources in place for the go-live, and that the education and training provided has sufficiently prepared the users for using the new system.

Ideally, the Collaborative Intervention structure is in place from the beginning of the project. These six critical stages serve as a guide as to when to conduct project assessments and what to look for. However, if the structure is not in place from the beginning of the project, then these critical stages will also serve as a guide for conducting an assessment at any point in time during the project.

Assess

Your next step in the Collaborative Intervention process is to know what to assess. There are many elements to consider in this assessment. Having a strategy to investigate and determine what the issues are is critical before you can effectively deal with them.

Collaborative Intervention

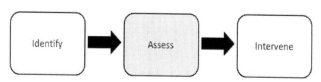

The assessment stage focuses on what is required to

identify the warning signs or trouble indicators.

You begin by asking questions such as these—and listening to the answers:

- Are the conditions right for a train wreck?
- Are we looking forward to see if danger lies ahead or are we heads-down managing tasks and not looking at the big picture?
- Everything is on track—the lights are green. What is there to worry about?

Often, with a large-scale project team, all the members focus on their particular task or rely on what is on paper while not looking deeper. Your role is to investigate further. Ask how the project team feels. Do they sense imminent danger? Is there a general air of disillusionment? Do they have a sinking feeling in their gut?

At each project stage, the assessment focuses on digging into project issues, cross-referencing documentation, and interviewing stakeholders to identify the warning signs in terms of expectations, time frames, and work streams.

The Collaborative Intervention assessment is composed of seven steps:

1. The expectations meeting
2. Review project documentation
3. Cross-reference documentation

4. Interview key participants
5. Determine areas of concern and recommendations
6. Review findings with key participants
7. Final report/areas for follow-up

Step 1: The expectations meeting. Each assessment begins with an expectations meeting. This is a meeting conducted with all the key project participants. At this meeting, the expectations for the assessment are discussed and agreed upon with all parties present. In addition, you should discuss the timeline for the assessment of documents that are to be reviewed, the people to be interviewed, and the assessment review process itself. Obtain agreement on all these points and you will have set the independent tone for the assessment.

Step 2: Review project documentation. After the expectations meeting, the next step is to collect the relevant project documentation for this particular phase of the assessment. Based on the phase of the project, this documentation may vary. For example, during the project planning phase, the documentation may consist of the statement of work, the project charter, the resource allocation plan, the detailed project plan, and the potential change management plan. Your purpose in reviewing the documentation is to gain an understanding of the project direction and the documentation that has been in place to guide the project, as well as to gain an understanding of project direction without having to conduct in-depth interviews about the project with each team member.

Step 3: Cross-reference documentation. After the project documentation has been reviewed, the next step is to cross-reference the documentation. The interventionist should cross-reference documentation to ensure that there is consistency among project deliverables and to identify the gaps that may occur in expectations, costs, resources, and budget, as well as to identify potential solutions. For example, during the procurement process many parties may be involved with writing the statement of work, or the statement of work may have varied from the original request for proposal. This happens frequently because the statements of work are often transitioned from the procurement and/or sales team to the legal team to the delivery team. Because of these handoffs, it is always a good idea to go back and cross-reference documents to make sure that you're buying what you intended to buy, since scope and delivery assumptions are often changed and added during negotiations.

Step 4: Interview key participants. After conducting a thorough review and cross-reference of project deliverables and documents, it is a good idea to interview the people who wrote, approved, and signed off on the documents. By interviewing key participants, the interventionist can determine if the project vision has been successfully translated into project execution. In addition, interviewing key participants helps the interventionist identify potential budget roadblocks, political concerns, or other constraints that would not be apparent by just reading the project deliverables. Information gained in these interviews is critical for understanding the complexities of the relationships among the parties involved in the project as well as for understanding what has and has not been successful in past projects within the organization. Interviews are also a great tool for uncovering people's fears and concerns and for gaining an understanding of the project goals. Without conducting interviews, the interventionist is left without a mechanism to build relationships with key project stakeholders that will allow for downstream issue resolution.

Step 5: Determine areas of concern and recommendations. After all documentation has been reviewed and cross-referenced and all key participants interviewed, the interventionist now has the information needed to develop the areas of concern for this assessment. Based on the project phase, the number of issues and areas of concerns will vary; however, the issues identified will represent gaps in terms of requirements, expectations, cost, budget, or resources. It is the responsibility of the interventionist not only to identify these issues and areas of concern, but also to provide recommended solutions.

Step 6: Review findings with key participants. After the interventionist has developed a list of concerns or recommendations, it is time to review the findings with the key project participants. This process is actually done twice. First, the findings are reviewed during informal discussions held individually with the key participants to ensure that nothing has been misinterpreted in the point in time assessment and to make sure that the key participants are briefed on the findings prior to a meeting of all stakeholders. This informal discussion with key participants prior to the formal meeting permits the interventionist to gauge the team members' reactions to the findings as well as to preliminarily discuss solutions. This also provides the key participants with time to research findings that they may not have been aware of or to brainstorm solutions prior to the formal meeting. The second time the findings are presented to key participants; everyone should be informed and aware of all of the issues and be prepared to discuss solutions. By being prepared in the first discussion, the participants have already bought into the recommendations and solutions. If they disagree, the interventionist can be prepared to defend the concerns and recommendations.

Step 7: Final report/areas for follow-up. As a final step in the process, the interventionist documents the point in time assessment by summarizing the process for the assessment, the findings, and the recommendations into a final report. This document marks the completion of the point in time assessment for this project phase. However, the final report serves as the input for the next point in time assessment. This is important because leftover action items or unresolved issues from the previous phase should be high on the interventionist's list for the next point in time assessment. Unresolved issues from a previous phase will be included in the documentation review, and interviews for the next point in time assessment will provide continuity between project phases to ensure that project failure points do not continue to go unaddressed.

Intervene

In the last stage of Collaborative Intervention, your role is to present the findings of the assessment and to intervene in order to make necessary project changes.

Collaborative Intervention

The Collaborative Intervention process outlines **how** to intervene by presenting the findings of the assessment and working with the project team to develop an implementation plan to address them.

Just as in the movies, the hero or heroine is aware that disaster is going to occur and must figure out how to stop it. The same is true for the enterprise project team. The project manager, a functional leader, or a key stakeholder may see the train wreck ahead but doesn't know how to stop it. And that's where the collaborative part comes in. Who can stop a train wreck within your organization? Is it one person, two, an executive, a vendor, or a team composed of all of them? More than likely it is the team. And to stop the wreck or have the train change direction, you need the buy-in of multiple people and departments. It is the interventionist's job to bring the warning signs to the attention of the stakeholders, propose a solution, and facilitate its implementation.

Case Study Part I

Trouble at FirstCorp

The executive committee meeting

The first time Jenny met Bill Parker was in the bi-weekly executive briefing. She was FirstCorp's project manager and responsible for implementing the financial applications that Bill would be using to run his operations. Needless to say, Jenny was nervous. Hired from a big-name consulting firm to lead the system implementation, her life was starting to settle down. Jenny had recently married and wanted to start a family—it was time to get off the road. She had worked on big implementation projects before, maybe not with this particular ERP application, but how hard could it be?

Let me tell you… it is really hard, Jenny said to herself. This project is a disaster. No one seems to be in charge and those who are "in charge" are indecisive. Cindy, the executive sponsor, is distracted by a new merger/acquisition. The software that was chosen for the implementation will not perform the business functions as promised by the vendors during the vendor selection process. CYA Partners, the consulting firm leading the implementation, has implemented this software three times before, but from talking to the consultants on the project, the first two implementations did not go so well. IT is freaking out about the timeline and the users are in revolt.

Jenny knew that she was walking into a meeting that was anything but routine. On the agenda was a discussion to change the go-live date, again. Rumors were running rampant that management was going to kill the project. Plus, at this meeting Jenny would meet the new controller, Bill Parker, who had just become her new boss.

Needless to say, Jenny was apprehensive...and downright worried. She found herself wishing she were back at her old job, on vacation, or even out sick. At the moment, the stomach flu sounded appealing. But most of all, she wished that things had been done differently.

Jenny straightened her shoulders and walked into the executive committee meeting. She took her seat and, once again, wished she were on a faraway island. Seated around the conference room table were the executive team members, whom she thought could not be more clichéd:

> *Bill—the new FirstCorp controller, and Jenny's new boss.*

> *Brett—the stubborn IT director, who always sat with his arms crossed while demanding that business requirements be defined for every request.*

> *Mary—the overly nice HR VP, who was always smiling and seemed out of place during the technical discussions, but who was willing to negotiate solutions.*

> *Bobby—the well-dressed executive partner from Coleman, Young and Alexander, LLP, (a.k.a. CYA*

Partners) the systems integration consulting firm, a man who always appeared tan and rested—which was at odds with his habit of dozing off during meetings.

Joining Jenny on the project management team:

Tim—Jenny's counterpart and the project manager from CYA Partners, Tim is well intentioned and competent, but a bit hamstrung by the inexperience of the consultants assigned to the project.

Janice—the charming change management and education lead. Janice had been the project manager for several past projects and was close to retiring. Since she was having a hard time grasping the complexities of the new systems, she was assigned to lead the change management and training effort for lack of other qualified candidates. Jenny was brought in to replace Janice as overall project manager. Janice didn't hold this against her, though, and actually took Jenny under her wing for guidance when she could. In all actuality, she just wanted to retire.

And absent again today:

Cindy—the COO and executive sponsor. Bill, Brett, and Mary all reported to Cindy and at the end of the day Cindy had the final word and everybody knew it. Nothing could get done without Cindy's approval—which wasn't hard to get if she could be found. Cindy was leading the integration of FirstCorp's latest acquisition and as a result was absent again today.

Jenny wondered if anything would change because Bill was now in their midst, but it quickly became apparent that was not to be the case. As usual, Tim began the meeting by jumping right into the status report and issues log as if continuing a previous meeting. The finger-pointing started immediately as Tim mentioned that IT was behind schedule on development. Brett reacted by crossing his arms and proclaiming that IT was behind due to the fact that the business side kept changing the system requirements.

"Here we go again," Jenny muttered.

"We keep changing the requirements because the BusinessWare software is not functioning as promised and the consultants lacked the knowledge to conduct a proper fit-gap analysis," Tim replied, looking to Bobby (who was starting to nod off) for support.

The discussion lobbed back and forth for another five minutes, when Bill stepped in. "So what is BusinessWare's position on this, Jenny?" he said.

"BusinessWare's position is that the system is functioning as designed and they have asked us to log a case. I wish it was a better situation—but *apparently we're stuck in tech support hell," Jenny replied.*

"Have we escalated the issues? Where is our account manager?" Bill inquired.

"Probably on the golf course," replied Brett, as Bill looked at him in confusion, while everyone else chuckled.

"No, I'm serious," Brett clarified, "we don't see too much of our account manager except when he occasionally drops by to take Cindy to lunch or the other executives golfing at the country club."

"I have been getting some voice messages from BusinessWare, but it's never the same person," Janice added. "I'm not even sure why they are calling me."

"Look," Bill responded. "I know I'm new here and a lot has happened to get us to this point and that there are questions as to whether this project should even continue. Well, the bottom line is this: FirstCorp has invested a great amount of time and effort into this implementation and is realizing that the project will not bring the anticipated returns. However, we may be too far down the road to turn back and be able to recover. Given the imminent merger, if this project does not succeed, we may need to clean house. If we can't get this software implementation back on track, all of our positions here are in jeopardy."

Bill continued. "Because I have some history with projects like this, Cindy has asked me to intervene. For the next two weeks, the executive committee is putting the project on hold while we take a closer look at where the project is in the implementation lifecycle, conduct an assessment, and determine if and how to get it restarted successfully.

"I will be holding a meeting at eight a.m. tomorrow morning to set expectations for the assessment," Bill stated, adding, "meeting adjourned—and for God's sake, somebody wake up Bobby!

"Jenny, can you please stick around for a few minutes? I need to speak with you," asked Bill.

Jenny slowly closed her project notebook. "Sure, Bill. I'm wishing for a way to make this project succeed."

"No wishing required, Jenny," Bill grinned. "Let me show you exactly what I mean by intervention."

Assessing the point in time

"Jenny, I bet this isn't the way you envisioned meeting your new manager," Bill said, after everyone else had left the room.

"No, not exactly," she replied. "You know I've only been here at FirstCorp for six months myself."

"Yes, I know. You have a good reputation here, and I need your observations to help me figure out how we got into this situation," Bill said. "I've talked with *some of the members of the executive team and they are legitimately concerned about the health of this project and our ability to successfully implement the systems."*

"Honestly, I'm concerned too. We've all been wishing for the proverbial decoder ring to decipher what is really happening in the project," explained Jenny. "We've been running on gut feeling, which makes it hard to communicate to the executive committee. As it is, they won't even make a decision unless Cindy is present. And she is never here. It makes everyone feel that she doesn't care."

"Oh she cares all right," Bill quickly said. "However, she is consumed with the merger and the CEO has said that is her top priority. That's why she asked me to step in."

"That makes sense," Jenny responded. "So how can I help?"

"Since you are fairly new to the project, you don't have the history and battle scars that Mary, Brett, and Janice have," Bill explained. "I need you to give me an update of where we are in the project."

"Sure, no problem. We're about to finish the development phase and begin testing," Jenny said.

Bill thought for a moment. "So if things were going according to plan, we would be getting testing and training ramped up to test defects and to start the process to gain user acceptance through testing, training, and communications, right?"

"Exactly," responded Jenny. "But that isn't the case. I've been thinking about this nonstop lately, trying to figure out how we got to this point."

"So what is your prognosis, Jenny?"

"I think we've made mistakes from the very beginning," Jenny related. "Instead of properly defining all the requirements, we decided we needed a new system for general ledger, accounts payable, and purchasing because our current homegrown system could not be upgraded. We did requirements analysis just for those modules and came up with a budget."

"Well, it sounds like things got started on the right track..." Bill began when Jenny interrupted him.

"I agree, but please remember, I hadn't joined the project team yet," Jenny reminded him.

"OK, got it," grinned Bill. "Please continue, Jenny. Remember, I'm not here to evaluate your performance, I just need to know how we got into this situation."

"Fair enough," Jenny took a deep breath and jumped in. "From what I can tell, the project team had a

good methodical process for the first three financial modules, but then things started unraveling.

"First, the billing department got involved because they needed a new system to track and bill for project costs, so the team figured as long as we were buying a financial package, then the billing and project costing modules should be added to the mix," Jenny said. "After a discovery session with billing, it was realized that a lot of the information needed for project costing to feed billing was in our time entry and payroll systems, which also needed to be upgraded along with the rest of the HR applications for personnel and benefits tracking. However, time was slipping away and we failed to do our due diligence for the other modules, because we figured if we purchased software from one of the leading ERP vendors, they would have this functionality covered. So in the end, we just increased our project budget to cover the additional costs."

"Did the timeline change?" Bill questioned.

"Kinda, but we still need to meet the project deadline," Jenny answered.

"OK, so what happened next?" asked Bill.

Jenny went on. "Each group went back to write up their requirements and we scheduled the vendor demonstrations. Under pressure to meet our timeline, we did not have all the requirements when *the vendors came in. So we went through the demonstration and picked the software we liked the best—the BusinessWare modules—based on what we knew. A few other firms in our industry use BusinessWare software packages and those references checked out, so the team figured the risk was minimal."*

"How did you choose the Integrator," Bill inquired, "and what is the deal with that narcoleptic Bobby?"

Jenny smiled. "Bobby lives next door to Ted, the CEO, so that should tell you a few things," she explained. "His firm, CYA Partners, has done a number of projects with FirstCorp, so they know our business. In addition, BusinessWare provided a list of three system integrators—and CYA Partners was on the list. We got proposals from the other two firms, but let's be honest about it: Bobby's firm had the inside track and won the business."

"So how are they doing?" Bill looked up from his rapidly expanding notes.

"OK," Jenny spoke slowly. "Not everything is their fault. They have some good people and some not so good people. On the downside, they don't have enough knowledge of the BusinessWare software, but this stuff is so new I'm not sure anybody does. On the upside, they are responsive to our requests if a team member is not working out and they will not

hesitate to tell us when the project is behind schedule because of items we are responsible for."

"Hence the friction between Tim and Brett," Bill observed.

"Exactly," Jenny said.

Bill pushed back his chair from the conference room table and began to pace the room.

"So let me summarize what you've shared with me to make sure I understand the situation," he began. "First, before the official implementation began, the requirements were not properly defined. Next, the software and services procurements were loose, so we're not even sure we have the right packages. Third, there are going to be gaps between the software capabilities and the business requirements, the extent of which we are starting to realize six months later, and finally, we aren't sure we allocated enough time, resources, and money to the project in the first place."

Jenny nodded. "Yep, that pretty much sums it up."

"OK, so was it about this time that you joined the project team?" Bill queried.

"Yes, I came on board right after all the contracts were signed and started the planning phase," Jenny explained. "Tim was on board as well and together

we developed the project charter and a detailed project plan. Given the procurement processes, I found several gaps, mainly in the area of change management and training. Since we didn't have the budget to pay the consultants for this piece of the project, we decided to do it in-house and assigned Janice as the project manager for the change management area."

"Does she have any experience in change management and training?" Bill asked.

"Some experience from her past projects," responded Jenny. "But I am not sure she—or the rest of the team, for that matter—fully understood the magnitude of the changes until we completed the design phase. Janice is a good project manager and can get things done if she has the right people. I guess we just aren't sure that she does."

"So you finished planning, closed some gaps between the statement of work and project plan, and began development, right?" Bill asked.

"Right," Jenny said, "except IT could not stabilize the demonstration environment in time for the design session. It was a comedy of errors. We couldn't get connectivity to the new servers in the conference room. Brett had to step in and stabilize the environment, but not before we lost two weeks in the process."

Jenny continued. "And it only escalated from there. Once we started the design sessions, some sessions went well and others were like opening Pandora's Box. We began to realize that we had never defined business requirements before and we had built our processes around the previous system. Since we needed to continue to define requirements we did not anticipate, we had to schedule additional meetings, extending the design phase. To make matters worse, the extension was during the HR Benefits open enrollment period. Because of this conflict, we weren't sure we had the right people from HR involved. I think this will probably come back to haunt us during testing."

"It probably will," Bill said. "OK, Jenny. I think that's enough for today. I have to give Cindy an update this afternoon and I'm starting to get a headache. I want to thank you for the input and your candor. I'll see you bright and early tomorrow morning."

As she left the conference room, Jenny didn't know what to think. Did I say too much, too little? Did I throw people under the bus? I can't tell. I actually have a headache too, hey... maybe it will turn into a stomach virus and I can miss the 8:00 a.m. meeting!

"I know, I know, just wishful thinking," she said out loud to no one in particular. [11]

Section 2—Conducting Project Assessments

Overview

This section provides a guide for conducting assessments at each of the six critical project stages. In order to successfully intervene at each critical project stage, the interventionist must combine the knowledge from the first phase of Collaborative Intervention: Identify, *or knowing when to intervene,* with the second phase: Assess, *or knowing what to look for.*

Collaborative Intervention

Identifying the Point in Time: *When to Intervene*

As mentioned in the previous section, the six critical stages to intervene in a project are as follows:

1. During the strategy phase, before the business case is presented for approval and funding. The purpose of the first assessment is to address top management's commitment to the project, expectations, and requirements definition.

2. During the acquisition phase, toward the end of the vendor selection process, before vendors are finalized and negotiations begin. The purpose of the second assessment is to address the software and services selection and gaps between the proposed software and/or services and the business requirements.

3. Toward the end of the planning phase, after the initial drafts of the Project Charter, Detailed Project Plan, and Change Management Plans have been developed. The purpose of the third assessment is to ensure that there is a strong project management methodology in place, that the project has adequate resources, and that the timeline and scope are realistic.

4. Toward the end of the design phase, after the initial drafts of the System Design Documentation have been developed. The purpose of the fourth assessment is to ensure that there are minimal gaps between the software and the business requirements, that the organization understands the impact of the change, and that the project has adequate resources allocated.

5. The fifth assessment should be conducted towards the end of the development phase. Its purpose is to ensure that the project management methodology for testing is in place, that the impact of organizational change is being addressed, and that the proposed education and training plans will meet user requirements.

6. The final assessment should be conducted towards the end of the testing and training phase. The purpose of the sixth assessment is to ensure that top management is committed to the project for the system cutover and the next phases of the project, that there are adequate resources in place for the go-live, and that the education and training provided has sufficiently prepared the users for using the new system.

Ideally, the Collaborative Intervention structure is in place from the beginning of the project. These six critical stages serve as a guide for when to conduct project assessments and what to look for. Collaborative Intervention provides project assurance throughout the implementation. However, if the structure is not in place from the beginning of the project, then these critical stages will also serve as a guide for conducting an assessment at any point in time during the project.

Assess: *What to Look for at Each Point in Time*

The Collaborative Intervention assessment is composed of seven steps, which are repeated in each of the Six Critical Project Stages outlined in the previous section. These steps include:

1. **Conduct expectations meeting.** This step is the same for each phase of the project. However, the attendees may change for each phase.

2. **Review project documentation.** The documentation will change based on the project stage.

3. **Cross-reference documentation.** Double-check the accuracy of each document against the others. The cross-reference will change based on the documentation for that stage.

4. **Interview key participants.** Find out what each individual is really thinking about the project and weigh the results against the overall project status. The interview questions will vary per project stage.

5. **Determine areas of concern and recommendations.** Focus in on common areas of concern and ideas for corrective courses of action. The areas of concern and recommendations will be based on the results of steps 2 to 4.

6. **Review findings with key participants**. Discuss the results of the intervention process with key individuals involved.

7. **Final report/areas for follow-up.** Hold a meeting to present the findings and determine areas for follow-up.

Putting It All Together

Because the intervention process is repeated at several critical points in time throughout the project, it makes sense to combine the first two steps in the process to describe when to intervene with what to look for at each critical project stage. The following section outlines each of the six critical project stages: how to assess project health through reviewing and cross referencing project documentation, stakeholder interviews, and addressing common areas of concern revealed through the intervention process.

Assessment #1—Determining Strategic Expectations

Validating Expectations

Once I was involved in a study for a company where, due to a long and painful transition to an ERP system, the chief executive ordered a study to determine whether the organization had chosen the right system. Sounds pretty straightforward, right? Not.

As it turned out, the project manager and the stakeholders each interpreted the purpose of the study differently. Their questions betrayed their confusion: Should we validate what we purchased? Should we look at new systems? Were there other systems and processes we missed? This disparity in viewpoints led to a debate as to what the project team was trying to accomplish.

These debates continued and were present at almost every project meeting. To me, the solution seemed obvious—go back and validate the purpose of the study to make sure that the CEO's expectations are being met. The problem was that the project manager and stakeholders did not have a good relationship with the CEO. They were fearful of going back to the CEO and asking the purpose of the study. They didn't understand the importance of that one step that could validate the project, so it never happened. Therefore, the results fell short of expectations and the team was not given another chance to make necessary system improvements. Untold time and money were lost in this case... not to mention the loss of improvement of business processes that the new technology would have brought to the enterprise.

Lesson learned? Validate expectations—starting at the top.

Strategy Phase Overview

Since the first assessment is conducted during the strategy phase, let's take a closer view of what the organization is trying to accomplish and clarify what you should look for. At this point in time, be sure to understand both the business drivers and what business problems the organization wants to solve. Is it the ability to make better business decisions by streamlining a process or having better access to information? Is it updating old technology platforms in order to improve competitiveness? Or is it a complete technology transformation to take the business to a global level? Understanding the overall organizational strategy is paramount to a successful first assessment, which is conducted during the strategy phase, before the business case is presented for approval and funding.

Common Issues Identified During the First Assessment

The strategy phase often starts with tactical issues such as a system replacement, outdated technology, or poor business processes. As problems are examined further, the team determines that the issues are larger than expected and further study or an assessment is required. What may have started out as a fairly straightforward project led to a complex project as people stepped back and looked at the impact on the larger organization. The first question to ask is: *Did you conduct a needs assessment?* The answer to this question, as well as the quality of the requirements as defined in the needs assessment, if conducted, will provide some of the first clues to the project's overall health.

In fact, consider these key findings regarding the quality of requirements definition:

- Companies with poor business analysis capability will have three times as many project failures as successes.
- 68 percent of companies are more likely to have a marginal project or outright failure than a success, due to the way they approach business analysis.
- Companies pay a premium of as much as 60 percent on time and budget when they use poor requirements practices in their projects.
- Over 41 percent of the IT development budget for software, staff, and external professional services will be consumed by poor requirements at the average company using average analysts versus the optimal organization.[12]

In addition to defining the project's requirements, the strategy phase is the time to understand what is driving the project time frame. Is it a business event? Additional support cost? Unsupported technology? Understanding the time frame requirements is critical to the overall project, as well as what drives the scope and the resources to be set aside for the project. Finally, expectations need to be set, communicated, and understood from the beginning.

Another common issue that can linger through an implementation is a lack of understanding the executive expectations. Failure to validate the expectations of the executive sponsors nearly always spells trouble for the project. Are the timetable expectations realistic in terms of industry standards and what is standard for the organization? If the organization is well run and has a history of project success, then aggressive time frames may be appropriate. On the opposite end of the spectrum, if the organization does not have a good history of project success, then the timeline may be inappropriate and the organization may need to rely on outside expert assistance to mitigate risk.

Conducting the First Assessment

The purpose of the first assessment is to engage top management, make sure requirements are properly defined, set expectations, validate time and cost estimates, and validate the methodology (or lack of).

The first assessment should be conducted during the strategy phase and should follow the following steps:

1. **Conduct Expectations Meeting**
   Purpose: To set the expectations and timeline for the point in time assessment.

   Who should attend: The decision makers from the various project entities internal to the organization (executives, business owners, and technology). If external partners are engaged and relevant, then they should be included as well.

What to expect during this phase: In reality, the strategy phase starts with tactical issues such as a system replacement, outdated technology, or poor business processes. As problems are examined further, the team determines that the issues are larger than expected and further study or an assessment is required.

2. Review Project Documentation
During the first assessment, the following project documentation should be reviewed for completeness:

The **Needs Assessment:** This is a document that outlines the current state of an organization, its desired future state, and an evaluation of alternatives and recommendations of how to achieve the future state. The Needs Assessment should consist of:
- Description of the current state or "as-is" process and system.
- Description of the challenges with the current process and system.
- Business requirements of the proposed solution.
- Technical requirements of the proposed solution.

- Impact of the change the proposed solution(s) will have on the organization.
- High-level fit gap between the proposed solution(s) and the proposed processes, systems, or organizational changes.
- Analysis of alternatives with pros, cons, and recommendations for moving forward.
- A Business Case analysis that should include the project budget for software, hardware, infrastructure, consultants, training, personnel and ongoing support costs, with cost justification and Return on Investment (ROI) modeling.

The **Implementation Plan:** This is a document that outlines how an organization is going to implement the desired future state outlined in the Needs Assessment. The Implementation Plan should consist of:

- High-level timeline for implementation to include procurement, implementation, and rollout.
- Resource requirements—project team, consultants, and additional full-time employees (FTEs).
- Training required for the project team.
- Estimated budget to include software, hardware, infrastructure, consultants, training, and personnel.

- High-level change management approach.

3. Cross-Reference Documentation

After the documentation is reviewed it should be cross-referenced to determine if there are:

- Consistencies in the overall methodology for moving forward.
- Gaps in functional and technical requirements.
- Interdependencies between proposed requirements: business process, current software system version, hardware / software compatibility.
- Dependencies between timelines and business events.
- Potential roadblocks due to organizational structure.
- Organizational gaps between users skill sets and the impact of the pending changes

4. Interview Key Participants

After the documentation has been cross-referenced, the following stakeholders should be interviewed: executive-level project sponsors, the business owners, project managers, and other key project participants.

Sample interview questions include:

- What are the business drivers of this initiative?
- What has been your process to get to this point in time?
- What are your expectations? Please define success.
- How have similar initiatives in the past been handled? What was the result?
- Are you concerned that any key groups are not involved in the project? If so, who?
- What is the current process for decision-making? Who is accountable?
- What issues and concerns do you have at this point?
- What other events are occurring in the organization that may have an impact on this project?

Assessment #2—Closing the

Procurement Gap

Techie-Speak Can Be a Good Thing

One of the most unbelievable project experiences I've been involved in was a situation where the business owners rushed to buy software without first validating that the IT organization could support it. In this case, a financial team spent a good deal of time defining the business requirements and meeting with software vendors to purchase a new customer billing application. After a thorough evaluation and due diligence, the group proudly purchased the software—confident they had made the right choice.

The next step? The team met with IT to install the product and start the implementation. To their horror, they discovered that the new software ran on a technology platform that was not supported by the IT organization. Someone failed to validate the system with the techies first.

Lesson learned? Validate the system with IT before you buy it.

Overview of the Acquisition Phase

In the acquisition phase, you still have your executives involved—they set the direction for the project. But now the project team is charged with finding and buying the software and services needed to implement the change. By now the organization should have a project manager on the team and someone from the purchasing function. The project manager is interacting with the business side as well as the technical side to make sure that all of the requirements are met.

Common Issues Identified During the Second Assessment

The strategic plan and the needs assessment plan developed in the previous phase now need to be translated into software and services that you will purchase to fulfill the business requirements. In most cases, during the Request for Proposal (RFP) process, the project manager assembles the requirements by meeting with the business/functional staff for the business requirements and with the technical staff for their technical requirements.

In some cases, the software vendors have been selected before all the system and technical requirements have been completely validated. This can be problematic in sorting through the best match of business requirements and system capabilities.

Organizations often rush to buy software or services before completely defining and validating all the requirements. Because software purchases are often viewed as technology enablers, not business improvement enablers, buyers rush to see the software demonstration without having a clear definition of what they want to purchase. This allows the software vendor, not the buyer, to drive the buying process. Your organization should only move forward with the software acquisition after validating that it will deliver what is required.

Things you need to consider during the acquisition phase include the following questions:

- Vendors have their own software strategies and limitations; were these explored before the organization committed to a solution?
- Is the vendor solution comprehensive—i.e., includes training, support, etc.?
- Were the executives involved in the evaluation stages to get vendors interested in participating as well as assuring a good fit?
- Can you get budgetary estimates prior to issuing the RFP so that when you get a cost proposal, you're not shocked at the price?

- Will vendors commit to a time frame that fits your organization's needs?

At the end of the day, you need to make sure that the organization has clearly understood and communicated all of the acquisition requirements, both functional and technical, from executives, business owners, technical owners, finance, and training. And make sure that the expectations set in the strategy phase are matched by the technical and functional realities of the chosen system. If there are discrepancies between the planned and the actual, such as how much the system will cost or the length of time it will take to implement, you need to reset expectations.

Conducting the Second Assessment

The purpose of the second assessment is to evaluate the software and services selection and address the gaps between the proposed software and/or services and the business requirements. The second assessment should be conducted during the acquisition phase, toward the end of the vendor selection process, before vendors are finalized and negotiations begin, and should follow the following steps:

1. Conduct Expectations Meeting

Purpose: To set the expectations and timeline for the point in time assessment.

Who should attend: The decision makers from the various project entities internal to the company (executives, business owners, and technology). If external partners are engaged and relevant, then they should be included as well.

What to expect during this phase: The strategic plan and the needs assessment plan developed in the previous phase should be translated into software and services that will be purchased to fulfill the business requirements.

2. Review Project Documentation

During the second assessment, the following project documentation should be reviewed for completeness:

The Procurement Plan: This document defines the process for the procurement of the goods and services required for the project. The Procurement Plan should consist of:

- Requirements validation
- Consultation with the finance or budget department
- Request for proposal development

- Vendor proposal evaluation process, to include:
  - Response time frame
  - Vendor demos & presentations
  - Site visits
  - Reference checks
- Vendor proposal scoring methodology for an overall response (technical and financial)
- Final selection process and award notification

The **Request for Proposal (RFP):** This is a formal document requesting proposals for goods and services needed for the project. The RFP should include:

- An overview of the procurement
- The steps in the procurement process
- The point of contact and process for vendor questions
- The procurement time frame
- Legal requirements
- Vendor qualifications (mandatory, minimal and preferred)
- Project background, scope statement, and anticipated time frame
- Project requirements or product specifications
- Proposal response guidelines for technical and financial response
- Request for vendor references
- Additional project/product information to assist in vendor response

- Sample contract/terms and conditions

Vendor Contracts/Statements of Work: The final contract is the document that binds the vendor to deliver the project and/or product and outlines the legal terms and conditions of the relationship. Since detailed issues regarding service delivery will reference both the RFP and final vendor proposal, it is important to evaluate these documents to determine whether the selected vendor proposal:

- Addresses all the requirements of the RFP.
- Does not include any vague or unclear responses.
- Includes all assumptions for project timeline, resources, and scope.
- Outlines vendor and client roles and responsibilities.
- Details the proposed costs and change control process.

Because initial terms, conditions, and scope may change during contract negotiations, it is important to communicate these changes to the project team. In addition, it is also paramount that the project team understands the processes and time frames regarding deliverable review and acceptance, as these items are typically tied to vendor payment.

3. Cross-Reference Documentation

After the procurement documentation is reviewed, it should be cross-referenced to determine if there are:

- Consistencies within the RFP back to the requirements, timelines, and costs outlined in the procurement document.
- Gaps between the vendor proposals and the requirements requested in the RFP.
- Changes in scope between the contract/statement of work and RFP.
- Additional purchases, such as supporting software or hardware that will result from the selection of a particular vendor solution.
- Processes for interviewing the vendor account managers or project team.

4. Interview Key Participants

After the documentation has been cross-referenced, the following stakeholders should be interviewed: executive-level project sponsors, the business owners, project managers, and other key project participants.

Sample interview questions include:

- Describe the procurement process to date.
- How do you feel the process is going?
- What are your impressions of the vendors/proposals?
- Do you have past experience or relationships with any of these vendors?

- Are any key people missing from the procurement process?
- What are your concerns about the process?
- What are your concerns moving forward?
- What other events are occurring in the organization that may have an impact on the project?

Assessment #3—Aligning the Troops

When a Gap in Expectations Becomes a Chasm
Let me tell you about a project where Collaborative Intervention would have been a real lifesaver. An enterprise-wide business process documentation project faced three significant challenges:

- A long delay between the procurement and start of the project
- Unforeseen budgetary issues that required scope changes
- Changes to the key project team members (sponsor and project manager) during the project.

In addition, expectations regarding the deliverables were not in alignment between the client and the software vendor. Both had different interpretations of the same wording in the statement of work. Although there were some discussion and agreement between the project managers, the differences in interpretation were never accepted by the team. The gap in expectations further widened when the client project manager left the organization for a new position and the team held their ground on their original interpretation. Since it was too late to intervene in the failure issues that had persisted throughout the project lifecycle, the gap in expectations became too wide to bridge and the project resulted in unfulfilled expectations for the organization, vendor, and consultant.

Lesson learned? To effectively intervene, make sure you understand the expectations of each key player and act before the gaps become too wide to bridge.

Overview of the Planning Phase

The third point in time assessment takes place during the planning phase. At this point, the project team is putting together the project methodology, the project plan, and the resource requirements, making the strategy more tactical. Who is involved? A much bigger project organization chart exists now. It's composed of technical, functional, change management, and training project managers.

Common Issues Identified During the Third Assessment

During the planning phase, gray areas are like pools of

quicksand that await the unaware. Given the chain of events that usually occurs during software acquisitions, it is likely that there are several gray areas because the project scope usually changes as part of contract negotiations. A common procurement strategy is to ask vendors to quote all possible services from which the buyer will pick and choose. These lines often blur during long negotiations, and team members may not remember what was discussed or may confuse discussions between different vendors. At the end of the day, it is vital to remember that what is in the contract is the only thing that counts. The contract is transformed into the Statement of Work or Project Charter.

At this point, you need to make sure deliverables are properly defined. The planning stage is also where the project scope is turned into the detailed project plan, the document that will guide the tactical implementation containing timelines, work breakdown structures, resources, and dependencies. It is critical at this stage for the interventionist not only to validate that project structure and governance, work streams, timelines, and resources are in alignment, but also to identify all the dependencies between timelines, resources, and work streams. Ask the tough questions: Will everything come together on time? Are there scheduled routine business events that will pull resources away from the project? Is there an unrealized dependency that will affect project scheduling?

Although the real answers to the these questions will play out over the project, it is the interventionist's job to look forward into the implementation to make sure the project work streams are properly aligned. The interventionist needs to pose tough questions early on and request concrete answers. Common questions may include: Who is responsible for change management? Is this included in the scope? When will a key decision be made? You need to recognize that vague answers to direct questions are always a red flag and that sometimes answers may not be available. If that is the case, then the questions need to be asked continuously through the point in time assessment until the answers are firm.

This is often the case with change management issues. If you have been involved in system implementations long enough, you know that change management services are often misunderstood by buyers. Because the scope is hard to define, many organizations take on change management themselves to save on consulting fees. To further hamper success, change management activities often start during the development phase, late into the project. To increase the odds for a successful outcome, the best practice is to begin change management discussions early in the project life cycle in order to set and align expectations. This approach lets you rely on resources that are available to participate in planning and design and to ensure proper deployment and work stream alignment.

Conducting the Third Assessment

The purpose of the third assessment is to ensure that there is a strong project management methodology in place, that the project has adequate resources, and that the timeline and scope are realistic. The third assessment is conducted toward the end of the planning phase, after the initial drafts of the Project Charter, Detailed Project Plan, and Change Management Plans have been developed, and should follow the following steps:

1. Conduct Expectations Meeting

Purpose: To set the expectations and timeline for the point in time assessment.

Who should attend: The decision makers from the various project entities internal to the company (executives, business owners, and technology). If external partners are engaged and relevant, then they should be included as well.

What to expect during this phase: Assessment at this stage is important because the procurement of software and corresponding services has been put into motion. You are at a crossroads from which it will be difficult to backtrack. This is a time when the statements of work, project charters, and detailed project plans are developed. This is also the point in the project where the vendor sales team hands off the project to the delivery team. Now is the time to determine if the services contracts are gap-free, completely in alignment with the requirements of your organization, and, most importantly, contain no gray areas.

2. Review Project Documentation

During the third assessment, the following project documentation should be reviewed for completeness:

The **Project Management Plan or Project Charter** is a document that defines in detail how the project will be executed and should contain the following:

- Accurate translation of the scope of the project from the contract/statement of work.
- High-level timeline for implementation to include procurement, implementations, and roll-out.
- Resource requirements (project team, consultants, additional project staff).
- Training required for the project team.
- Project management structure: meeting structure, issues resolution process, change request process, governance structure, organization chart, and risk plan.

The **Detailed Project Plan** or **Work Breakdown Structure** documents the tasks required to execute the project and should contain the following:

- The detailed work breakdown structure of project tasks translated from the Statement of Work
- Resource assignments
- Key milestones
- Task dependencies
- Estimated task start and finish dates

Project Management Documents, which will be used on an ongoing basis for project management. Typical project management documents consist of:

- Status reports, issue logs, risk mitigation plan.
- Critical issues or items of concern.
- Any potential risks.

The **Change Management Plan** documents the approach for implementing the organizational change required as part of the project. The Change Management Plan should include the following:

- Stakeholder / sponsorship analysis
- Organizational change impact assessment
- A communication plan
- Training and support plan

3. Cross-Reference Documentation

- After the procurement documentation is reviewed, it should be cross-referenced to determine if there is:

- Transfer of scope, resources, and timeline from the Implementation Plan developed in the Strategy Phase.
- Consistency between the Project Charter and the Detailed Project Plan.
- The presence of all work streams as identified in the Project Charter and previous point in time assessments in the Detailed Project Plan.
- Integration of change management tasks into the Detailed Project Plan.

4. Interview Key Participants

After the documentation has been cross-referenced, the following stakeholders should be interviewed: executive-level project sponsors, the business owners, project managers, and other key project participants. Sample interview questions include:

- What are your impressions of the project team?
- Are any key people missing from the project?
- What are your concerns about the project?
- How do you feel about the overall timeline?
- What other events are occurring in the organization that may have an impact on this project?
- What do you see as the impact of change on the organization?
- How do you plan to address it?
- Is project communication adequate?
- Are decisions being made in a timely manner?

Assessment #4—The Design Disconnect

Balancing the Project Workload

You know, it seems like every project I have been involved in has had some form of the design disconnect. One case in particular comes to mind... during the design phase for a large system conversion; it became evident that although there were twelve client employees assigned to the project, four project team members were involved in the majority of the tasks. To illustrate the point, I took the project organization chart from the Project Charter, mapped the team members who were actually participating in the project, and pointed out where there were gaps.

In defense of the people who were not contributing, it wasn't their fault. They were being pulled in multiple directions by conflicting priorities. It was definitely time for an assessment to keep the project on track.

I asked for a meeting with the lead executive, and after a frank and honest discussion about the disconnect within the project team resources, he freed several people from the conflicting priorities to focus on the project, freed the people who were contributing to the project from non-project related activities, and even identified some new resources that added value to the project team. The result was a more focused and dedicated project team, which, despite the design disconnect, delivered the system on time, on budget, and with user acceptance.

Lesson learned? Intervention works when you take the opportunity to make it happen.

Overview of the Design Phase

The fourth assessment point occurs in the design phase.

At this stage, you are at the project team level—team leaders and the people who will be using the system. Their input was solicited into the design of the system, and, at this point in time, there's a lot of flexibility in moving things around. What often happens, as the project team creates documents and validates software fit/gap, is that the project team may find that the requirements were not fully understood or there may be interdependencies that weren't uncovered until now. You may discover other issues that need to be addressed that were not dealt with as part of the software purchase.

You may experience an event like W2s, Open Enrollment, 1099 processing or other operational events that cause the design phase to go longer and impact development schedules as a result.

Common Issues Identified During the Fourth Assessment

1. Resources. Do you have enough resources to complete the project? Go back to the project plan or charter and determine who was to be committed to the project.

- Are they the right people?
- Are they torn between their regular job and the project?
- If they've been marked as a resource, are they really contributing anything? If not, it is a liability.

2. Time frame. Typically, project managers develop the overall timeline for a project up front, with stakeholders for development tasks that will be finalized after the design phase. The questions related to project failure issues that arise after design includes:

- Is the time frame appropriate?
- Has the design phase been extended due to extra meetings?

- Have additional requirements been identified that will require development and testing?
- Will you try to make up time in development and testing?
- Will you change the go-live date?

3. Scope and Focus. In many cases, key people in the design phase are the same people who are going to be assisting with the testing and training. In the rollout, they are the ones who know the product, the business functionality, and how the system needs to be configured to be effective within the organization. They are the validation input, the training input, and the message makers. In short, they are invaluable to your project's success.

- Who are your key people?
- Do you have enough key players?
- Are they overcommitted and causing bottlenecks?

Also, at the conclusion of the fourth assessment, it is appropriate to begin a discussion about the go-live date. Ask yourself realistically, is it still in reach? Even if everything is on track, it's a good exercise to have these discussions so that they will not be taboo later in the project when they may be necessary.

Due to the "disconnects" that occur during the design phase, be sure that scope, timeline, and resources are all in alignment. Because you have the Collaborative Intervention® structure in place, it is easier to communicate with the top level of management with a dialogue that lays out what is taking place and why that may extend the timeline of the project. At this point, you have everybody you need to solve the problem available and there may be multiple solutions: Resources can be added to the project, changes can be made to the go-live date, or changes can be made to the scope of the system rollout in the form of a pilot or phased launch.

Conducting the Fourth Assessment

The purpose of the fourth assessment is to ensure that there are minimal gaps between the software and the business requirements, that the organization understands the impact of the change, and that the project has adequate resources allocated. The fourth assessment should be conducted towards the end of the design phase, after the initial drafts of the System Design Documentation have been developed, and should follow the following steps:

1. Conduct Expectations Meeting

Purpose: To set the expectations and timeline for the point in time assessment.

Who should attend: The decision makers from the various project entities internal to the company (executives, business owners, and technology). If external partners are engaged and relevant, then they should be included as well.

What to expect during this phase: At this stage, you are at the project team level—team leaders, users, and the people who will be using the system. Their input was solicited into the design of the system, and, at this point in time, there's a lot of flexibility in moving things around. What often happens, as the project team creates documents and validates software fit/gap, is that they may find that the requirements were not fully understood or there may be interdependencies that were not uncovered until now. You may discover other issues that need to be addressed that were not dealt with as part of the software purchase.

2. Review Project Documentation

During the fourth assessment, the following project documentation should be reviewed for completeness:

The **System Design Document** is a document that translates the business requirements into the design for system configuration. The System Design Document should include a:

- Fit-gap assessment of business requirements/processes for the proposed solution, to include a plan for system configuration, required development, and reports and interfaces.

- Percentage of requirement gaps identified by priority and level of effort.
- An overview of the entire hardware and software architecture and data design, including specifications for external interfaces.
- All lower-level detailed design specifications of the business product, such as general system characteristics, the logical and physical data model, user interfaces, and business rules.
- Requirements Traceability Matrix, which describes how the system design will satisfy the functional, business, security, and technical specifications in the Requirements Document.
- Definition of the release strategy.
- Data conversion, interface, and reporting strategy and design.
- Change requests based on discovery conducted as part of the design.

The **Detail Project Plan** (identified in Assessment #3) which should consist of:
- Plan performance on schedule, percent complete, ability to complete, and changes to the date and timeline.
- Resource availability and utilization by the project.

- Level of effort and timeline for the development phase.

Project Management Documents (identified in Assessment #3), which should consist of:

- Status reports, issue logs, risk mitigation plan.
- Critical issues or items of concern.
- Any potential risks.

The **Change Management Plan** (identified in Assessment #3), which should consist of:

- Stakeholder analysis.
- Change impact assessment.
- Leadership impact, awareness, and participation.
- Identification of new behaviors.
- Communication and training plan.

3. Cross-Reference Documentation

After the design stage documentation is reviewed, it should be cross-referenced to determine the following:

- Does the percentage of software gaps equal the amount predicted in the procurement phase?
- Has the timeline for the design phase been completed on time?
- Has additional scope been added to the development cycle?

- Has the go-live date been extended?
- Are the resources listed in the project charter engaged in the project based on the original time commitment or have changes occurred?

4. Interview Key Participants

After the documentation has been cross-referenced, the following stakeholders should be interviewed: executive-level project sponsors, the business owners, project managers, and other key project participants.

Sample interview questions include:

- What are your concerns about the project?
- Do you still feel that the overall timeline is reasonable?
- What other events are occurring in the organization that may have an impact on this project?
- Who is not engaged in the project but should be?
- Based on the design session, do you see additional changes or impacts to the organization/users?
- How do you plan to communicate change?
- Are decisions being made in a timely manner?

Assessment #5—Evaluating Testing and Acceptance

Playing Go-Live Chicken

Ever played the game of chicken? If you have, you'll recognize it in this case of a $20 billion organization that was implementing a major ERP financial system upgrade. I was part of the project management team that met every week with our project sponsor to discuss status. We had started out with a long project timeline... but now we were behind schedule due to the sheer size of the upgrade and the complexity of the organization's database.

It's seven o'clock at the Monday morning weekly meeting. Before we have even taken our seats, our executive sponsor opened with, "Are we going to make the cutover date?" To which each of the project managers responded, "Yes, but there are issues with…" You can fill in the blank. Training. User acceptance. Business process interruption. Resource allocation. Etc., etc.

The game of go-live chicken can be an expensive one. Because the executive sponsor felt that the cutover date was more important than the readiness for the cutover, end users were not fully trained to use the system. We made the date, but as a result, accounting entry errors skyrocketed and the organization's financial accounting function was compromised until all the errors could be corrected.

Lesson learned? Being an interventionist is not for chickens.

Overview of the Testing and Acceptance Phase

By the time you reach the testing phase, it should be apparent as to whether or not the project is going to come in on time and make the go-live date.

During this phase the interventionist should also review testing logs to evaluate and prioritize defect resolution. By having a Collaborative Intervention® framework in place, holding discussions regarding your findings and any impact on the go-live date should be expected and productive.

Common Issues Identified During the Fifth Assessment

If your project is on track, the questions to ask at this

point in time assessment include:

- Will the organization/users be ready for the new system and what is the acceptable level?
- What have past acceptable levels been?
- What was successful in terms of communication and training?

Given that project scheduling is always negotiable and that it is nearly impossible to make all users happy, the interventionist should work with the project team to identify ways to improve user acceptance. For example, including more users in acceptance testing, holding additional classes, on-site/side-by-side user coaching and support during cutover, post-go-live conference calls, or impromptu training sessions all have a positive impact on end user acceptance.

In addition to acceptance, the interventionist should also address user support for the cutover and transition period and work with the project team to anticipate user support needs:

- What type of issues will the users face in the new system?
- Who will they call?
- Where can they get answers?
- Can we handle the call volume?
- Should we establish an online help desk?

As they say, you never get a second chance to make a

first impression. If the users' first impression is frustration reinforced by further frustration because they can't get help, then the system will be poorly perceived—no matter how well the project was implemented.

Conducting the Fifth Assessment

The fifth assessment should be conducted towards the end of the development phase. The purpose is to ensure that the project management methodology for testing is in place, that the impact of organizational change is being addressed, and that the proposed education and training plans will meet user requirements.

1. Conduct Expectations Meeting

Purpose: To set the expectations and timeline for the point in time assessment.

Who should attend: The decision makers from the various project entities internal to the company (executives, business owners, and technology). If external partners are engaged and relevant, then they should be included as well.

What to expect during this phase: At this time if you have followed the project assurance methodology, things should be on track. But if the project is falling behind, then you need to focus on getting the project back on track by evaluating the pillars of project management: time, resources and scope.

2. Review Project Documentation

During the fifth assessment, the following project documentation should be reviewed for completeness:

The **Detailed Project Plan** (as identified in Assessment #3), which should consist of:

- Plan performance on schedule, percent complete, and the ability to complete.
- Changes to the go-live date and timeline.
- Resource availability and utilization by the project.
- Level of effort and timeline for the development phase.

Project Management Documents (as identified in Assessment #3), which should consist of:

- Status reports, issue logs, risk mitigation plan.
- Critical issues or items of concerns.
- Any potential risks.

The **Test Plan** is a document that outlines how the system will be tested and should consist of:

- Definitions for all the types of tests to be carried out: unit, functional, integration, system, security, performance (load and stress), user acceptance, and/or independent verification.

- Test Case Specifications, which describe the purpose and manner of each specific test, the required inputs and expected results of the test, step-by-step procedures for executing the test, and the "pass/not pass criteria" for determining acceptance.
- Description of the roles and responsibilities of individuals involved in the testing process and the traceability matrix.
- Description of the resources needed for the hardware and software environments documented in the test plan.

The **Training Plan and Schedule** (as defined in Assessment #3 in the Change Management Approach), which should consist of:

- Description of the goals, learning objectives, activities and information that are to be provided to stakeholders who use and/or support the software product solution.
- Complete and accurate documentation of the deployment of the software product.
- Schedule of key communications, messages, and delivery method for training and cutover preparation.
- Plan/schedule for the development of training materials.
- A list of the required training classes, trainers, and delivery methods.
- A list of the users who need training.

5. The **Communication Schedule** (as defined in Assessment #3 in the Change Management Approach), which should consist of:

- Schedule of key communications, messages, and delivery method for training and cutover preparation.

3. Cross-Reference Documentation

After the project documentation is reviewed, it should be cross-referenced to determine if:

- There are any outstanding development items that are preventing testing and/or training from moving forward.
- The system will be ready for the development of training material.
- The timelines for communication and training are in alignment.
- There any significant defects or show-stoppers.

4. Interview Key Participants

After the documentation has been cross-referenced, the following stakeholders should be interviewed: executive-level project sponsors, the business owners, project managers, and other key project participants. Sample interview questions include:

- What are your concerns about the project?

- Do you still feel that the overall timeline is reasonable?
- What other events are occurring in the organization that may have an impact on this project?
- What are other opportunities to communicate changes to the organization? What has worked well in the past?
- Who is not engaged in the project, but should be?
- Based on the testing sessions, do you see additional changes or impacts to the organization/users?
- How do you plan to communicate change?
- Are decisions being made in a timely manner?

Assessment #6—Transition and Optimization

Overestimating User Skill Sets

Training and change management continue to be the Achilles's heel of enterprise software implementations. One cause of training and change management failure is that project teams routinely overestimate the technology skill sets of end users.

Let's face it, implementation team members are fairly tech-savvy and often assume end users will pick up concepts quickly because they do. I have been involved in several projects where the project team's mentality was "people book their airline tickets online and shop at Amazon, so they should be familiar with web-based systems or self-service functionality." These same team members were shocked to find out during training that the users struggled with Microsoft Office and basic web navigation.

When developing baseline expectations in change management and training plans, don't forget that there are still a lot of people who dial the eight hundred numbers to buy airline tickets, write checks at the grocery store, and don't shop online. Project teams should use these as baseline assumptions and work their way up from there by assessing the technical skills of the end users. Change impact assessments should be conducted early on in the project to properly asses end user skills and provide the necessary time to develop different levels of training based on end user competency.

A one-size-fits-all approach only works if everybody is on the same level—which is rarely the case in large organizations. If different training levels are not an option due to time or budget constraints, consider offering pre-training in basic system concepts or informal learning labs for those users who need it. Additional training offerings, learning labs, or small-group help sessions should be made available post go-live, since that is when such help is often needed the most.

Overview of the Deployment Phase

The sixth and final assessment point is transition and optimization. You're ready to ice down the champagne. The system has gone live. The users are up and running.

But is it really time to declare victory? A more realistic approach may be to celebrate the achievement, but know that in some cases the work is just beginning.

Common Issues Identified During the Final Assessment

During the final point in time assessment, the interventionist should ensure that the project is properly closed out and transitioned to operations, that knowledge transfer from consulting resources has taken place, and that deferred scope is prioritized. In reality, many project teams are too burned out to properly wrap up a project and the significant effort put forth on the project is soon forgotten.

Project team members will often urge the interventionist to communicate to the executive or steering committee the need to continue to have a collaborative structure post-go-live. Their reasoning is that once the project is over, the focus will shift to other things. Those of us who have been involved in enterprise software implementations realize that the project is never really over. As an integral part of an organization's infrastructure, the system continues to need nurturing, making it important to continue the collaborative process and structure post-go-live.

Conducting the Final Assessment

The purpose of the sixth assessment is to ensure that top management is committed to the project for the system cutover and the next phases of the project, that there are adequate resources in place for the go-live, and that the education and training provided has sufficiently prepared the users for using the new system. The final assessment should be conducted towards the end of the testing and training phase and consists of the following steps:

1. Conduct Expectations Meeting

Purpose: To set the expectations and timeline for the point in time assessment.

Who should attend: The decision makers from the various project entities internal to the company (executives, business owners, and technology). If external partners are engaged and relevant, then they should be included as well.

What to expect during this assessment: Since the system has just gone live. Now is the time to get to those pesky and unpopular tasks that the project team has been procrastinating on, such as documentation, change requests, production support processes, knowledge transfer, and deferred scope.

2. Review Project Documentation

During the final assessment, the following project documentation should be reviewed for completeness:

The **Detailed Project Plan** (as identified in Assessment #3), which should consist of:

- Plan performance on schedule, percent complete, and the ability to complete.
- Changes to the go-live date and timeline.
- Resource availability and utilization by the project.
- Level of effort and timeline for the cutover and transition phase.

Project Management Documents (as identified in Assessment #3), which should consist of:

- Status reports, issue logs, risk mitigation plan.
- Critical issues or items of concern.
- Any potential risks.

Test and Training Outcomes (as identified in the Test Plan in Assessment #5), which should consist of:

- Test plans, test cases, test files, and/or test data defined and developed.
- The evaluation of performance metrics.
- Defect tracking and issue resolution process.
- Documentation that acceptance testing has been completed and that the outcomes verify readiness for training and implementation.
- A summary report created at the end of the test phases that completely documents the overall test results, including summarizing the test activities and describing variances, including the identification of unexpected

problems and/or defects that were encountered.

The **Communications Schedule** (as defined in Assessment #3 in the Change Management Approach), which should consist of:

- Schedule of key communications, messages, and delivery method for training and cutover preparation.

The **Production Support/System Cutover Plan** outlines in detail the activities required to turn on and support the new application. It should consist of:

- A detailed cutover plan to include schedule and resources for go-live weekend.
- A plan for end user support for cutover and transition period.
- The information necessary for the operations, help desk, and support staff to effectively handle routine production processing, ongoing maintenance, and identified problems, issues, and/or change requests.

The **Knowledge Transfer Plan** documents how knowledge will be transferred from the project team members to ongoing operations. It should include:

- Listing of knowledge, skills, and abilities that need to transition from the project team or consultants to operational roles.

- Identification of resources that possess the knowledge, skills, and abilities who will need to transition and who they will be transitioned to.
- Listing of roles, tasks, and schedule that needs to transition from the project team or consultants to operational roles.
- Identification of who performs various roles and tasks and who these roles and tasks should be transitioned to.
- Schedule/timeline for the knowledge transfer process.
- Identification of a process to verify and validate that project knowledge has been adequately transferred.

3. Cross-Reference Documentation

After the transition and optimization documentation is reviewed, it should be cross-referenced to determine if:

- The system has been thoroughly tested. Are there any significant defects or show-stoppers?
- The majority of users have been trained on the new system.
- The users are aware of the go-live date and support plan.
- There will be extra support for end users during the cutover and transition, based on the amount of change impact.

- The contractors and consultants are scheduled to roll-off. If so, when? Is this in line with contracts?
- There is a plan to address deferred scope and a release schedule for enhancements.

4. Interview Key Participants

After the documentation is cross-referenced, the following stakeholders should be interviewed: executive-level project sponsors, the business owners, project managers, and other key project participants. Sample interview questions include:

- What are your concerns about the go-live?
- Do you feel that the team and organization are ready?
- What are the plans for the cutover? Is everyone aware of the plan?
- What other events are occurring in the organization that may have an impact on this project?
- How do you plan to address deferred scope?

Case Study Part II

The Project Assessment

The expectations meeting

Well, it's 8:00 a.m. and no stomach virus, Jenny thought to herself. Guess I'm going to have to gut it out and sit through this meeting. Given the gravity of the situation, everybody else had also arrived early—including Bobby, who was armed with an extra-large coffee. Everyone apprehensively took a seat around Bill's conference table overlooking the FirstCorp campus.

"I think everyone knows why we're here today," Bill began. "As I mentioned yesterday, Cindy asked me to step in and assess the current situation and to determine a plan to get the project back on track. I've already spoken with many of you informally. As a result, I know that there are many reasons we are in this situation—some of which may be beyond your control.

"Here's what will happen next," Bill continued. "Over the next ten days we'll be conducting a project assessment and, if necessary, an intervention. Jenny and I will be leading this process. Our goal is to present the assessment findings to Cindy next Friday. We'll begin this process by reviewing the relevant project documentation and cross-referencing it to make sure we have covered all the gaps. In addition, we'll meet with each of you individually to get your input on the situation and ideas for potential solutions. From these documentation reviews and one-on-one interviews, we'll generate our recommendations."

"Any questions?" Bill looked around the group. His question was met with silence. Someone coughed.

"OK, starting with the action items." Bill went down his list. "Tim and Jenny, I will need a copy of the following documents: the original needs assessment, the project strategy, the budget, the RFP for software and services, the vendor proposal, the project charter, the detailed project plan, the statement of work, the project issues log, the risk plan, and system design documents.

"In addition, I'll be contacting each of you for interviews to get your input, perceptions, and suggestions," Bill said. "Thanks, everyone. And Jenny, I'll see you in my office at one p.m. to get started."

"Can you believe this guy?" Tim said as we walked out of the room. "I know he is new, but he doesn't have a clue of how things get done around here."

"You know, Tim, I think I'm going to give him the benefit of the doubt," Jenny said.

"Obviously, you have to," Tim replied. "He is your manager. But frankly, I just don't get it—we just completed the project audit from that third-party firm. Wasn't that enough?"

"I don't know, Tim," she replied. "In all actuality, the audit only looked at our project management methodology. As a result, we tightened a few things up in terms of status reporting and project governance, but

the audit didn't address the other issues we are having with the software or change impact. There was no root cause analysis."

"Well, even if we do address the root cause, it's not like Cindy is going to make any changes," Tim challenged. "We all know how she is."

"We'll find out, won't we, Tim?" Jenny glanced at her watch. "Let's just get started on pulling the documents together that Bill requested. It's looking like I've got some long days ahead of me."

The documentation review

"I believe this is everything," Jenny said as she piled the last stack of documents on the conference table in Bill's office.

"Great," Bill grinned as he pressed the button on the coffee maker. "Coffee is brewing, let's get started."

For the next five hours and four cups of coffee, Bill and Jenny poured through various project documentation from the first four phases of the project—strategy, acquisition, planning, and design. Finally at 5:00 p.m. they wrapped up.

"Let's regroup early tomorrow morning," Bill said. "Is seven a.m. good for you?"

Jenny nodded, sending her husband a text message to alert him to her early morning schedule.

As she drove home, Jenny realized that listening to her favorite classical station was not as soothing as usual. In fact, she found herself gripping the steering wheel so hard that her fingers hurt. She couldn't help but think there had to be a better way. After all, she had completed her project management certification last year. This type of project derailment was not supposed to happen on her watch. Granted, she was not involved in the strategy and selection process, but she should have seen some of the warning signs when the project charter and work plan were developed. "Don't beat yourself up too much, Jenny," she said to herself as she pulled into the driveway.

It was a beautiful, crisp fall evening, so Jenny decided to go for a run to clear her head.

As she began her usual three-mile loop, she realized that her pent-up stress was making her run way too fast. She decided to slow her pace or the run would quickly become a short run and frustrating walk home. As her thoughts drifted back to the previous day's conversation with Bill when she was giving him the project update, it hit her like a ton of bricks. "We know what we have to do, but not necessarily how to do it!" she exclaimed. Wait a second, did I really say that? It sounds like one of those overly simplified clichés developed by some consultant writing a how-to book—we know what we have to do, but not how to do it.

In fact, Jenny realized, it was true. Once the train left the station, everyone felt it was too late to address the issues for fear of personal or team failure. They were so focused on making the date that they rushed through the procurement process. They thought there were going to be gaps in the software but didn't know how to address them. They knew that they needed BusinessWare to step up and resolve their critical issues, but they couldn't get the issues escalated. They knew that Cindy made all the decisions, but not how to get the issues in front of her. And they subconsciously knew that there were potential time bombs waiting to explode. When the bombs eventually did explode in the form of the project being placed on hold, their collective fate was placed on this assessment.

As Jenny rounded the final corner and headed down the hill toward her house, she felt a little better. Bill was providing an objective opinion and identifying the real issues. The main question: Could he execute the solution?

Carbs, caffeine, and clarity
She stopped at the donut shop and picked up a couple of bagels.

"Nothing like a few carbs to go with the caffeine," she said to Bill, when she ran into him in the elevator on the way to his office at seven the next morning.

Bill chuckled. "Make that a double—I brought donuts, too." So much for calorie containment, Jenny thought. Good thing she had gone for a run last night.

Bill and Jenny continued the document review throughout the day, making copious notes and identifying key issues on the white board. At the end of the second day, they had identified several themes.

1. Not everything is a disaster. We have some good people on the project team and we have a sound project management methodology and structure. We did a good job of defining the requirements for the core financial modules, which was the original scope of the project. The related project tracks or "swim lanes" are progressing with few issues.

2. Our expectations and timeline were flawed from the beginning. We underestimated not only the effort and complexity of the procurement process and contract negotiations, but also how long it would take to get our development environment for the design sessions in place. We painted the IT department into a corner to get us a development environment and, because they underestimated the effort as well, they committed to an unrealistic timeline. In addition, the early phases of the project went past their completion date, yet we did not change the target go-live date.

3. *The project team was stretched too thin. Proficient team members were involved in every meeting while having to continue to do their full-time jobs. Worse still, several of the people assigned to the project were not competent. They were offered to the project team because some of the operations managers did not want to give up their best people to the project.*

4. *We kept a good log of the issues. We just weren't able to get resolution of the issues either internally or externally. Internally, we presented our concerns and risks about the target date, lack of proper requirements, and misaligned project team members to the executive committee on several occasions, but with Cindy's lack of participation, there was a reluctance to act. Externally, we seemed to have no visibility with BusinessWare. You would think that because FirstCorp is a large, well-known company, the vendor would be concerned if we could not implement the software. The impact of bad press would be devastating to BusinessWare. In fact, there were several show stopper defects within the financial modules that would need resolution if the software was to be implemented.*

5. *Some of the software modules were definitely off track and behind schedule. HR was pulled into the project without the opportunity to think*

through their requirements. It appears that FirstCorp's business process and employee environment are a complex mix of unions, multi-national employees, hourly, part-time, and salaried employees—all with their own benefit mix and payroll schedule.

"So, what do you think?" Bill asked, at the end of the second long afternoon.

"Frankly, I wish we had gone through this exercise sooner," Jenny responded. *"On one hand, we probably could have prevented some of these issues before they occurred. Looking back, there definitely were some critical points in time that, if we had done an earlier assessment of the project, would have turned out differently and we'd be in better shape now. On the other hand, even if we had done the assessment, I'm not sure we had the structure and consensus to implement any changes. But one thing I do know is that everything is becoming a lot clearer now."*

"I agree," Bill said. *"Let's schedule the interviews with the other team members."*

"Let's start with interviewing Brett," Jenny said. *"To me, he seems the most skeptical."*

The interviews

Brett's office was tucked away in the back corner of the IT department, overlooking the parking lot. Brett was a portly guy who preferred short-sleeve shirts and enjoyed fishing. His office walls were lined with striped bass and trout mounted on wooden plaques. A gleaming brass trophy of a large catfish served as a hat rack for an Atlanta Braves baseball cap. Brett was not really happy with the project, but that was no surprise as he wasn't really happy with most things at FirstCorp. In his defense, IT did get a lot of requests dumped on them— always a crisis and at the last minute—and never a lot of thanks.

It was easy to see that Brett was increasingly becoming fed up with the constant requests from the project team —for greater access/security, more data refreshes, or more development environment.

"Tim and I have done our best to limit these requests," Jenny mentioned to Bill as they walked down the hallway to Brett's office. "But some were necessary, essentially always putting us at odds with Brett."

Once seated in Brett's office, Bill began the interview by asking Brett to provide his take on the project up to this point.

Despite the occasional profanities, Brett was conflicted. "I recognize that a lot of work has gone into the project up to this point and that some of the delays were a result of my people having to react to constant requests without really understanding their priority," Brett answered. "I'm OK with the progress being made with the financial applications, but the HR side is a damn mess—*struggling with requirements and constantly sending mixed signals."*

"To tell you the truth, I think the bigger issue is that BusinessWare isn't listening—or if they are, they aren't taking us seriously." Brett was becoming increasingly agitated. "My concern is fundamentally about the lack of response from BusinessWare. My suggestion is that I call Charles, the BusinessWare account manager, to set up a meeting or at least a conference call as part of this assessment."

Immediately Bill and Jenny agreed. They both knew that many of the outstanding issues could not be resolved without vendor support.

"Look, I know my job is on the line here," Brett stated flatly. "But I am convinced that the entire scope of the project cannot be implemented by the date scheduled. And I'll be honest with you, Bill, I'm skeptical of your ability to convince Cindy to take the recommendations of yet another assessment seriously."

Overall, Brett made it clear that he felt that FirstCorp had bitten off more than it could chew. However, Brett concluded by saying that while IT was supportive of the project; he wanted to make sure that the proposed solutions were realistic and implementable within the project time frame. Bill promised to review the assessment results and recommendations with Brett before meeting with Cindy. This made Brett feel a little better.

The next interview was with Mary from Human Resources. Mary's office was warm, inviting, and well decorated. It felt like a visit to her living room. Throughout her office were pictures of her family as well as posters and mugs from FirstCorp's HR recruiting campaigns.

When Bill and Jenny arrived, her two direct reports and the corporate counsel were in her office discussing a personnel issue in one of the plants. It did not sound good—people were going to have to be let go and they were anticipating potential lawsuits and press involvement.

They waited outside her office for at least fifteen minutes, until the door opened and Mary appeared.

"Mary, we can reschedule for a better time," said Bill.

"I doubt there will be a better time," quipped Mary. The usually cheerful and reassuring Mary was not here today; instead they met with the stern Mary, VP of HR, who was obviously stressed by the latest personnel crisis and not really happy with the software project.

She didn't really want to have to deal with Jenny and Bill right now, but she did not want to reschedule. Plus, she needed someone to take her frustrations out on.

"So Jenny, what's the latest with the software issues from the vendor?" Mary began the interview on the offensive. *"And has Brett figured out those technical issues yet?"*

"We're working on that, Mary," Jenny smiled in reply.

"You know what? Cindy is just going to cancel this project and we are going to go onto the systems from our acquisition of Parnew," Mary challenged as she looked at Bill. *"And in all actuality, it might not be such a bad idea. Parnew implemented a new HR system last year and it appears to be light-years ahead of where we are. I'm not even sure why you both are wasting two weeks with this assessment."*

"If you remember, Cindy has asked me to go through this process," Bill replied easily.

"Exactly, so that she has what she needs to stop this train wreck!" Mary shot back.

Jenny felt her stomach sink and heart rate jump as the interview continued. She could see Mary's assistant poking her head in, trying to get Mary's attention, because the division manager was on the phone.

"Well, I did speak with Cindy about the systems from the new company. Yes, they have some solutions in place, but not for all the modules we need. Our business is more complex than Parnew's in several significant areas," Bill countered.

"Who planned this project anyway? Who plans design sessions in the middle of open enrollment?" Mary paced the room, arms folded. "Our existing systems are getting the job done, so why are we involved in this project?"

"OK, I understand," said Bill.

"Look, that's all I have to say," Mary strode to the door and opened it. "I've got to deal with this other crisis right now."

"I thought that went rather well," Bill mused, as they left the HR department.

"Yeah, right," Jenny responded. "Mary's not usually wound this tightly. I think she feels dragged into this project and obviously she's dealing with some heavy personnel issues."

Next up on the interview circuit were the project consultants from CYA Partners. Bill and Jenny were anticipating some defensiveness—and they weren't disappointed. They met Bobby and Tim for lunch in the company cafeteria.

Both men were defensive of their position and tried to put the blame back on the FirstCorp project team. Obviously, they didn't want to admit being at fault, because CYA might then have to provide additional services on their dime to cover their insufficiencies. Or even worse, give FirstCorp a refund.

Tim pointed out that there weren't enough resources—or even the right resources—assigned to the project team. Bobby mentioned change management and training and offered to provide additional services in those areas. Funny, Jenny noticed Bobby always seemed to be about additional services.

Jenny did ask about a couple of CYA consultants who led the team astray in several areas of the project. She believed that they might not have possessed the level of experience that the firm originally proposed. She reminded them of their young consultant who didn't fully understand the difference between debits and credits and always got the plus and minus signs confused. And then there was the example of the consultants who were attending training for their assigned software modules after the fit-gap occurred. Saving the best for last, Jenny brought up their consultant who e-mailed the high-resolution picture of his boat with the subject line "For Sale" to the entire company—nearly crippling FirstCorp's e-mail server.

"OK," Tim acknowledged. "Maybe we are partially to blame for the situation." Bobby looked down at his empty plate.

"We really do want to make sure you succeed," Bobby admitted. "I know you joke that we get a lot of business because I'm Ted's neighbor, but you guys know Ted and his temper. It's not unusual for him to show up after work at my house when things aren't going well and rip

me a new one—even while my kids are playing video games in the next room. So tell me, how do you want to proceed?"

"Let us finish our process and make some initial recommendations," Bill said. "We'll meet with you again before talking to Cindy."

"In the meantime, I'm going to call Charles at the software company and make sure he knows what is going on here," interjected Bobby. "I don't think we can fix some of these functionality issues without him."

"I'd appreciate that," said Bill. "You should know that Brett is going to call him as well and suggest a meeting or conference call."

"I will do the same, Bill," Bobby grinned. "I think once Charles knows the situation, we will have his support."

The final interview was with Janice. A FirstCorp veteran, Janice had managed countless projects in the past, some good, some bad, but none as large or complicated as this one. She was the initial project manager for the strategy and acquisition phase and, frankly, was in way over her head. She had even told Jenny that this project was going to be her swan song into retirement, but it was turning out to be more of a holding cell.

In many ways, Janice represented the old guard—slow to grasp new concepts, but too valuable in organizational knowledge to be cast aside. When Tim and Jenny reported to the executive committee that they needed a change management and training lead, Janice was immediately selected. Looking back, it was clearly a decision made as a solution for what to do with Janice rather than one based on her qualifications for the change management job.

The interview with Janice was actually more of a monologue. She gave Bill and Jenny endless history lessons as to why things will never change as well as countless stories of the good old days at FirstCorp. On her office walls hung the proof—probably more than a hundred photos of Janice with every CEO and at every major function that the company had for the last thirty-five years.

Thirty minutes later, Janice paused. "You know, to be honest I really don't know much about change management and training, but I'm glad to be involved in the project," she said. "You won't find anyone else on the project team who is as loyal to FirstCorp as I am—it's just that this isn't the way I envisioned my career ending."

"Wowser," Bill said after the interview. "Janice really does have a lot of good experience. Obviously she is in the wrong position. I wish we could find a better way to use her skills."

"Me, too," Jenny replied sadly. "So what's next?"

They walked through FirstCorp's hallways back to their offices. "Let's have the conference call with BusinessWare," Bill said, "and then meet to discuss our findings."

When Jenny got back to her office, she found an e-mail from Brett inviting her and Bill to a conference call with Charles from BusinessWare. She forwarded the invite to Bobby and Tim so that they could all participate. The conference call was scheduled for 10:00 a.m. the next day in Brett's office.

The conference call

"Hello, Charles, are you there?" Brett pulled the conference call speaker closer.

"I'm here," Charles's voice crackled through the receiver, as Brett tapped on the volume button.

"Good," responded Brett. "I have Jenny, our project manager, Bobby and Tim from CYA Partners, and Bill, who is our new controller, on the line with me."

"OK, morning everyone. Bill, nice to meet you," Charles said. "Will Janice be joining us as well?"

"Thanks," Bill replied curiously, "no, Janice won't be joining us."

"OK then, on my side, I have asked Lisa to join us. Lisa is our new client executive assigned to FirstCorp," Charles stated.

"Welcome, Lisa," Brett replied. "Charles, you just said that she is our new client executive, but I wasn't aware that we even had a client executive. We thought you were the account manager."

"Well, in a sense, I am the account manager, but I actually handle more of the sales side," Charles explained. "Lisa handles the day-to-day issues."

"Charles, this is Jenny talking. Did we have a client executive before Lisa?" she asked.

"Well, actually this is a little embarrassing," Charles said, clearing his throat, "but as it turns out we have had a lot of turnover and re-orgs at our company. Originally, you had Mike as your client manager, then Francis, and then George."

"I have to say I'm a little shocked," Jenny responded. "Why is it we've never met with these people?"

Charles quickly replied, "I'm not sure how that can be—they've been in contact with Janice all along."

"Janice isn't the project manager," Bill stated.

"Well, if she's not, then who is?" Charles quizzed.

"Jenny is our project manager," Bill clarified. "She took over from Janice after the contract was signed."

Silence.

"Guess it's a good thing I'm new and that we are having this conversation," said Lisa, breaking the silence. "At least we have a clean slate to start working with."

"Yes, it definitely is a good thing," Jenny said, as everyone laughed nervously.

"Well, now that we've gotten the account manager relationships straightened out, what's up?" Charles asked.

"Go ahead, Bill," Brett said.

"Charles, we are having some issues with your software," Bill explained. "We're trying to get a handle on exactly how many problems exist, but according to Jenny and Tim, there are several show stoppers."

"Have you logged them with our Tech Support?" Lisa asked.

"Of course," Jenny replied, "but we aren't getting any resolution. And now Tech Support is telling us that the issues will be resolved in a future release. Frankly, we can't afford to wait. As Bill mentioned, there are a couple of show stoppers in there."

"Well, this isn't good news," said Charles. "Lisa, how can you help FirstCorp with this?"

"Jenny, if you can get me a prioritized list of your issues with the corresponding case numbers, I will see that these issues get properly escalated," Lisa said. "And we can have a daily call between us until the most critical issues get resolved."

"Works for me," Jenny said, deeply relieved on a couple of fronts.

"Let me tell you that I'm glad to hear that you are going to help us resolve these issues, Charles," Bill said. "But there's one more thing that you need to know. Cindy has asked me to conduct an assessment of the project to determine if we will keep moving forward with the implementation. We are presenting our findings to her next Friday. We need to make progress on this list before then. I also think it would be good for you to be at the meeting as well."

"Got it," said Charles. "We will make the issues a priority here at BusinessWare and we'll also be at the meeting next Friday. And please know that we're sorry for the confusion about Janice—we really thought she was your project manager."

"Jenny," interjected Lisa, "send me that list ASAP."

"Will do."

"OK," Bill said in closing. "We'll let Jenny and Lisa take it from here. Charles, we'll contact you with the meeting details once we have them."

"Sounds good. Talk to you later," Charles said, as he signed off the call.

"Can you believe that?" Tim asked incredulously. "We've had a client executive the whole time, but they were talking to the wrong person. Unbelievable!"

"Brett, thanks for setting this call up, it was obviously very helpful," Bill said.

"Yeah, thanks," Bobby chimed in. "So what happens next?" he asked, turning to Bill.

Bill thought for a moment. "Jenny and I are going to get together to summarize our findings. Then we'll have a meeting to discuss them as well as our preliminary recommendations before going to Cindy. I'll send you an invite once we can finalize a time."[11]

Section 3

Becoming an Interventionist

Overview

In the last stage of Collaborative Intervention, your role is to present the findings of the assessment and to intervene in order to make necessary project changes.

Collaborative Intervention

The final stage of the Collaborative Intervention process is to intervene. The Intervene stage outlines **how** to intervene by presenting the findings of the assessment and working with the project team to develop an implementation plan to address them.

Attributes and Behaviors and the Intervention Process

It doesn't take a rocket scientist to know that how you deal with people in difficult situations can be the most important component in project success. So far, you've learned about the critical intervention points and the point in time assessments that outline **when** to step in and **what** to look for at each step along the way.

In this section, we'll take a look at the art of the intervention—or the **how**—in the form of the attributes and behaviors of a successful interventionist, as well as at processes you can use for conducting project interventions.

The Attributes of the Interventionist

A successful interventionist has critical behavioral attributes that, when practiced together; generate intelligent oversight and project synchronicity.

An interventionist is: objective, analytical, strategic, and diplomatic.

Attributes of an Interventionist

Objective	Analytic
Diplomatic	Strategic

Be Objective

In order for an interventionist to objectively look at the project from the outside, you must have a healthy sense of both skepticism and realism. When you are conducting an assessment, you may be met with apprehension. It's human nature for people to feel threatened when their performance is being assessed. However, as a result, some project team members may overstate the progress of the project. The interventionist must remain objective: skeptical enough to dig deeper into the answers instead of accepting them at face value, while realistically assessing the situation.

By the same token, you must be careful not to be too skeptical and assume that the project team isn't competent and that the project is a total disaster. For the most part, too much skepticism creates an antagonistic relationship with the project team that is counterproductive. This is why the objective interventionist must balance skepticism with realism. Understanding the environment surrounding the project team is critical to building the trust necessary to develop collaborative solutions for live project issues.

On Objectivity
OK, let's start with the simple definitions of the two words. Skeptical—inclined to skepticism or having doubts. Realism—the tendency to view or represent things as they really are.

I was brought into the early stages of a large-scale business process improvement project to conduct an assessment—maybe too early—as the project was still developing many of the project documents such as the Project Charter and the Detailed Project Plan and Change Management Plan. I quickly discovered through developing my document checklist that many of the documents were still in the development process. Even some of the answers that I was seeking were still being discussed by the project leadership.

Skeptically, it would have been easy to assume that the

project was already in jeopardy because key documents and deadlines had been missed. But realistically, the client was doing further due diligence planning and budgeting to address some additional scope issues that had arisen.

Armed with objectivity, I determined that the project really hadn't yet begun. In fact, once the project documents were completed and the project timeline was adjusted—there were no issues at all.

Objectivity trumps assumption every time.

Be Analytical

The second attribute of the interventionist is to be analytical. Your primary task is to analyze information that is found in key project documents, that is taken from one-on-one interviews with people involved, and that is cross-referenced in the documentation. To perform these tasks, the interventionist must be analytical enough to decipher and track key project elements of the different stages of the project, ensure their consistency, and identify gaps and solutions.

A big part of being analytical is asking how. Many times project documents discuss **what needs to happen** but don't address **how it is going to happen**. A major reason for this is that project documents such as charters and statements of work are rarely developed from scratch, but rather are taken from previous projects and edited to suit the current project's needs. Another scenario for vague statements and project charters is that verbiage for a particular project area is copied from the vendor's proposal. Keep in mind that when a vendor is responding to the proposal, particularly for an area that they have a corresponding weakness in, the vendor's response will be nonspecific. Look closely and you will see that they respond with what they are going to do versus how they plan to do it.

The tactic of describing "the what" versus "the how" is often used by vendors and project managers to obtain sign off on documents or to get past a particular stage. This language can actually mislead the people who are reading the document because they assume the issues are being addressed just because there is a section in the document discussing what needs to happen. Without an analytical viewpoint, the how often goes unaddressed. By asking how something is going to occur, you should get a specific response. The failure to get a specific response is a definite red flag.

Being Analytical
Never trust anyone who says, "Trust me."

Many years ago I was a technical project manager for a large-scale Y2K project converting the client legacy system to a new client/server system. The main issue that I was concerned about was the printing functionality. The new technology allowed people to print both to the centralized printer and to local printers in their office. But there was a catch: To print to the local printer it had to be centrally set up and not just mapped from the user's PC, as was the case with printing documents and spreadsheets. As the project progressed, I kept asking our technical team lead how the printing would actually work. But the answer I kept getting back was "Trust me, users are going to be able to print both centrally and locally."

No one could give me the explanation of how the printing function actually worked. As a result, what was required to make it work was not even on the project plan.

Just ask how.

Being analytical means to get past what is going to occur and to start getting into how it is going to occur. This translates the idea into tasks. It is why the interventionist must continually ask how. In doing so, what you may eventually discover is that there are gaps between the concept and the reality of the implementation. These gaps result in a significant outlay of effort and time, which, by the way, are not represented in the project plan or budget. Identifying these gaps is the cornerstone of the point in time assessment.

Be Diplomatic

There is no doubt that diplomacy is critical to creating the environment for the intervention. Diplomacy helps you to communicate effectively in coaching the team to address and resolve issues. Consider this: An expert project manager may have the knowledge and analytical ability to identify the gaps in the project, but without diplomacy, the expert will have little luck in facilitating solution development and implementation.

The word diplomacy has connotations of government, in the sense of facilitating relationships between nations. This is similar to, albeit less formal than, the role of the interventionist. Just as a diplomat must understand the unique cultures and traditions of the countries involved, the interventionist must understand the dynamics of the culture and relationships within the organization, among departments, and between the vendor and the client.

At the heart of diplomacy is the ability to negotiate. It is easy for someone to act diplomatically and build congenial relationships, but oftentimes these relationships are only on the surface. To be truly diplomatic, the relationship must evolve from platitudes to mutual trust and respect. Keep in mind that during an intervention, you will be viewed with skepticism. Using diplomacy, it is your job to overcome that skepticism and build a respectful working relationship. Once mutual trust and respect have been established, the parties can work together to negotiate solutions.

Whether conducting a Collaborative Intervention or just working on a project in general, successful consultants are often the most diplomatic. In many cases, a consultant's experience and expertise may be similar to the client's. However, the client is bringing in the consultant to help solve the problem that they are unable to solve themselves. This usually happens because communications have broken down. The consultant's role is similar to a diplomat negotiating issues between opposing nations: It is to bring consensus and to help negotiate a solution while using your own experience to establish credibility as an expert. Without diplomacy, your ability to facilitate and build consensus for the solution will fail.

Be Strategic

The fourth attribute of the interventionist is to be strategic. Being strategic requires that you understand the problem, understand the project, understand the environment, and provide the context for the good plan. You must build solutions as well as develop and implement the plan for communicating the problem and resulting solutions. In a normal project audit, the deliverables often stop with the presentation of the recommendations. There is no strategy for how to implement the recommendations. Collaborative Intervention goes beyond this to create the approach to implementing the solutions by building a consensus among project decision makers that the solutions are necessary, and arriving at an agreement on the approach to implement the solutions.

Given the fact that gaps in the project identified through the Collaborative Intervention process may indicate deficiencies in some project areas, you will probably experience resistance or push-back as to the validity of your report and unwillingness to recognize and resolve the gaps. In order to address this resistance, the interventionist must think both strategically and diplomatically when presenting these issues in order to build consensus that the recommendations are necessary.

When talking about strategy, it is almost impossible not

to think in military terms. Almost all definitions of strategy refer to warfare, battle, or competition. And frankly, there are similarities to the interventionist's task. Just as a general or competitor must understand his opponent, you must understand the players involved in order to implement your plans. It is naive to think that the organization will just accept and implement your recommendations automatically. The interventionist understands the dynamics of the environment, the sources of power, the decision-making process, and their collective impact on the implementation of the recommendations.

In some cases, this may translate to holding more informal meetings, or, where sensitive issues are involved, private meetings with key executives.

Being Strategic

When you're in the middle of an intervention, there are only two types of discussions: public and private.

Once, during a business transformation project, I was involved with a project that was having issues with the resources on the project team. The people in question were three members of the client project team. It was a question of their level of knowledge of the business processes and the system functionality—as well as their time commitment to the project. I discovered this situation through assessment interviews with the client project manager on the vendor staff.

Due to the sensitive nature of the resource issue, my strategy was to discuss this with the client's executive sponsor in a private meeting. My goal was first, to create recognition that there was an issue, and second, to mutually assess the employees' contributions and performance on the project. While in this private session, the executive and I were able to develop a plan to replace and supplement project resources with people who were the right resources for the project and were committed full-time. By having a closed door, one-on-one discussion, I was able to address the resource issue and change project team members tactfully and without embarrassment to any of the parties involved.

Know when to close the door.

The Behaviors of an Interventionist

By now you know what a fan I am of "how" things are done. The successful interventionist will master personal behaviors in order to achieve the desired goal: listening, seeking to understand, humility, and compromise. Within the context of the four behaviors is their interrelationship. There is no hard stop where one behavior ends and another begins. For example, in seeking to understand an issue, you must listen well and carefully to what is said—and not said. In approaching a compromise, you need to disarm the natural oppositional response of resisting interference with humility.

This diagram shows the interrelationships of these four interventionist behaviors that I believe will net you the greatest return: listening, understanding, compromise, and humility.

Behaviors of an Interventionist

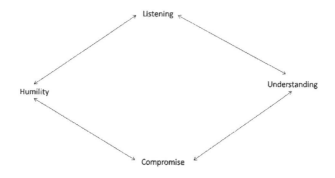

Listening

The first key behavior of the interventionist is listening. Many people do not actually listen to conversations or to what people are trying to communicate to them. This practice is described as active listening versus passive listening. An active listener is paying attention to the words that are being said, to the voice tone and inflection of the speaker, and to the nonverbal cues as well. Passive listening is when you hear the words, but rather than processing them, you're already working on the solution In your head.

There are consultants who believe that they have the answers to their client's problems before they walk in the door. While it's not unrealistic that the consultant, based on experience and knowledge, may have a pretty good understanding of what the issues are and what the potential solutions may be, he or she would be remiss by not actually listening to the client. Remiss not only in gaining a full understanding of the situation, but also in building the credibility and trust needed to establish the relationship and implement their solutions.

Understanding

Essential to the role of interventionist is understanding. It is important to try to understand the point of view of the person you are interviewing, the specifics of the project, and the dynamics of the overall organization. All these factors are not only critical in determining the current state of the project, but are also essential for developing a strategy to implement change.

As part of understanding, it is important to not only identify the role of the person and the project environment, but also to place yourself in that person's shoes. By asking questions designed to better understand another person's concerns, fears, and motivations, you will have a better sense of the reality of the situation. In addition, you'll earn credibility and respect with the project team members because of your interest in them and desire to understand their point of view.

The human factor is a common denominator in project failures. Having the behavior traits that allow you to really hear and truly understand what your project team members are telling you is a major step in intervening before failure becomes a reality.

Humility

Can you be an expert and be humble? The answer is a resounding yes. The third behavior of a successful interventionist is humility. Being humble in approaching the client's issues—without arrogance, impatience, or condescension—is essential to the Collaborative Intervention process. Because the interventionist is an outsider to the project, the organization, and the members of the team, coming into the situation with guns loaded will only cause people to withdraw from discussions or to resist you and any hope of solution. Bringing a sense of humility to the table creates the perception of being genuine—genuine in the sense that you are there to help identify and solve problems on the client's behalf and not for your own ego. As with the other behaviors, humility is crucial to establishing rapport. It creates trust by letting others know that you have their best interests at heart.

Compromise

Putting the behaviors of listening, understanding, and humility into action forms the final behavior of a successful interventionist: the ability to compromise. Previously, we discussed the importance of diplomacy and negotiation in reaching consensus among disparate groups. But reaching consensus is often not possible without the willingness to compromise. It is often the case that each party has to give up something to reach a solution. It can be any party in the discussion, including the interventionist, who may have to yield parts of his or her position to achieve consensus for workable solutions to project problems.

Behaviors

Many consultants believe that they have the answers to the client's problems before they walk in the door. Experience (or lack thereof) has given them the egotistic ability to think they can recognize the same situations in different environments. But the truth of the matter is that no two implementations are alike. There are unique factors, different influences, and distinct pressures that allow no categorization of a project—other than the type of technology being implemented.

Frankly, I'm often surprised by how many people don't actually listen to conversations or what people are trying to communicate to them. They're too busy listening to their own thoughts and formulating a response. I challenge you to put yourself in the other person's shoes and really understand what they are saying to you.

The only way to master the Collaborative Intervention is to master the fundamental behaviors of listening, understanding, compromise, and humility. And interestingly enough, I think you'll soon find yourself employing them in any situation where other people are involved.

The Intervention Processes

Now that we have discussed the successful attributes and behaviors of the interventionist, we can outline the process for communicating project issues, building consensus, and implementing solutions. The intervention process pyramid has three layers: building the foundation, navigating the organization, and implementing the solution.

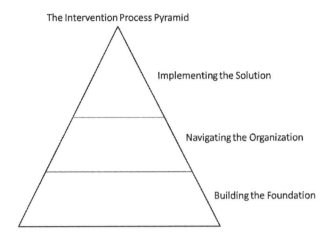

The Intervention Process Pyramid

Implementing the Solution

Navigating the Organization

Building the Foundation

Building the Foundation

All good relationships are based on trust and credibility. Trust and credibility are best established through a person's attributes, behaviors, and actions. If you have been selected to perform a project assessment, you should already have the experience and credentials needed for the job—in fact; this provides you with initial credibility. But if your attributes and behaviors fail to establish a rapport and relationship of trust with the project team, your credibility is all for naught. To build a foundation for successful intervention, you begin with attributes and behaviors that build trust and credibility.

The Intervention Process Pyramid

Implementing the Solution

Navigating the Organization

Trust & Credibility

Building the Foundation

Attributes & Behaviors

Navigating the Organization

Identify the Decision-Making Process and Sources of Power

One of my favorite terms related to successful project management is "navigating the organization." Project teams are complicated and may consist of a variety of players and participants, including, but not limited to, executives, project managers, team leaders, consulting executives, consultants, independent contractors, and vendor partners. All these people need to be pointed in the same direction for the success of the project. But how is this accomplished, who is in charge, and how are decisions made?

This information is crucial for the interventionist to know in order to be effective. The tricky part is that this information will vary from project to project and from organization to organization. You'll also encounter formal power versus informal power in the form of influence.

So where do you start? Here is a very effective (and possibly familiar) process for determining how decisions are made:

1. **Start with the obvious.** As simple as it may sound, start with the information contained in the project documents such as the needs assessment, project plan, or charter. These documents should contain at a minimum: the definition of project team members' roles and responsibilities, the organization chart, the issue resolution process, and the project governance structure.

2. **Validate the information through observations and interviews.** Ask questions such as, "Can you make that decision?" "Who made that decision?" "What is that person's role?" Once decision makers start to emerge, ask questions to determine who has influence, such as, "Whose advice does the decision maker seek?" or "What is their process for gathering information?"

3. **Observe how decisions are made.** As part of the assessment, attend a project governance

meeting or steering committee meeting. Observe the process and communication patterns of the executives. For some organizations, such as vendors or consulting firms, the process is easy to assess, as there is usually just one person in charge of the account. Inside an organization, the decision-making power will be harder to discern.

Good places to look for answers about how decision making occurs are internal politics, past success, and funding. Typically, executives who have had past project success will have the organizational credibility to either make the decisions or influence them. You also can't ignore who is funding the project, as well as the dynamics among internal departments. There are situations where CIOs, CFOs and HR VPs do not communicate with each other and, as a result, have completely different perceptions of issues and resolution. In cases like this, where stalemates exist, you may have to go higher, to find an executive who is not involved in the project to act as a tiebreaker.

From the steps above you should be able to map out the process required to start communicating issues and building consensus for issue resolution. However, use caution to always maintain your foundation attributes and behaviors. The sources of power can change quickly in the form of a resignation, reassignment, or retirement of a key project executive, leaving the project with an entirely new landscape. A good strategist will always use the knowledge of the power structure as protection against project failure due to unforeseen change.

After you have determined the sources of power, it is a good idea to rate the project team members based on their role in the decision-making process, the strength of your relationship with them, and their accessibility.

Each project team member should be rated according to the following criteria:

Decision Role
- Decision Maker
- Influencer
- Champion
- Negative Influence
- Team Member/Contributor

Relationship Rating
- Strong
- Moderate
- Weak

Accessibility
- Easily Accessible
- Accessible

- Inaccessible

Rating the team members along these criteria will help in developing a strategy for communicating your findings.

Conducting Mini-Briefings

Despite what you may think, people, especially executives, don't like to be surprised, unless the news is overwhelmingly good—like winning the lottery. Since it is unlikely that you will be delivering overwhelmingly good news, it is best that everyone is prepared and aware of any issues before the meeting with the group as a whole. The best way to accomplish this is through the mini-briefings.

The mini-briefing can be a scheduled event or informal conversation, where the interventionist provides an overview of the assessment and the potential recommendations. This pre-discussion serves several purposes:

1. **No surprises.** People have an opportunity to be prepared for a difficult discussion if necessary.

2. **Validate your findings**. It is possible that you may have misinterpreted situations or have been given incorrect information. If either is the case, then you will save yourself from an embarrassing situation and keep your credibility intact by validating your position ahead of time.

3. **Provide an opportunity to fix a problem**. Often times, executives may be unaware of a particular issue and the fix may be relatively simple. By providing them an opportunity to fix a problem, you are saving them from a potentially uncomfortable situation while building trust with that individual.

4. **Provide an opportunity to start thinking.** Whether it's about potential solutions or digesting your recommendations, getting everyone on the same page ahead of time helps when you get a group of executives together. If potential solutions are complicated, it is good for people to think through them before a meeting. It helps everyone to understand the solution and to determine the pros and cons, thus preventing rash decisions that may be pushed along by an executive in a position of power.

The Intervention Process Pyramid

Implementing the Solution

Conduct Mini-Briefings

Navigating the Organization

Identify the Decision-Making Process

Trust & Credibility

Building the Foundation

Attributes & Behaviors

Implementing the Solution

The final stage of the intervention process is implementing the solution. By this time, you have built the foundation of trust and credibility and navigated the organization by determining the decision-making process. Then you validate your findings through the mini-briefings. Now it is time to assemble the project team and sponsors in order to present your findings and develop the action plan for solution implementation.

Communicate the Findings

The project assessment report will most likely contain good and bad news. Since communicating bad or less than positive news to people is never easy, here are some guidelines:

1. **Soften the blow**. Use pre-meetings to inform everyone involved and avoid surprises.

2. **Set the stage**. First discuss your process and how you reached your findings. Let people know what documentation you reviewed and who you interviewed.

3. **Start with good news.** Positively acknowledge people's accomplishments, achievements, and cooperation in the assessment process.

4. **State the facts.** Pure and simple, without emotion or finger-pointing. To quote a popular phrase, *"it is what it is."* Mention (without names) any opposing views to or disagreements with your findings that you sensed from the mini-briefings.

5. **Ask for input.** Let people state their views if they disagree, but always focus on facts, not emotions.

6. **Present your recommendations.** There is nothing worse than someone who points out flaws without solutions. If it is a difficult problem with alternative solutions, outline them. If you truly cannot solve the problem, state that and lead a discussion to come up with solutions.

Negotiate Solutions

The final part of solution implementation is to negotiate solutions. It is probable that all your recommendations will not be accepted or possible given the parameters of the project. The key is to gain consensus that your findings have created legitimate concerns and need to be addressed. Any number of reasons—time, budgets, or politics—may prevent the implementation of the solution as you see it. Therefore, it is important to work with the executive team to acknowledge the risk and find alternative solutions to project issues. The solutions should be documented, added to the project plan or action item log, and reviewed at the next point in time assessment.

The Intervention Process Pyramid

Summary

The obligatory pyramid does a nice job depicting the process of communicating project issues, building consensus, and implementing solutions. Built on a solid foundation of attributes and behaviors, we can see not only the traits of a successful interventionist, but also the process required to be successful as well. In summary, the four attributes—objective, analytical, diplomatic and strategic—work together with the four behaviors—listening, understanding, humility, and compromise—to build the foundation for trust and credibility.

Trust and credibility help the interventionist ask the tough questions and observe behaviors in order to navigate the organization, map the decision-making process, and conduct the mini-briefings. Successful organizational navigations create the collaborative environment necessary for group communication and negotiations.

The Intervention Process Pyramid

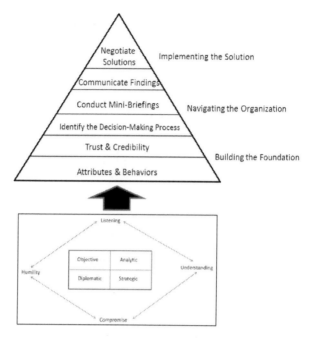

Attributes & Behaviors of the Interventionist

Case Study Part III

The Intervention

The review meeting: somewhere between a rock and a hard place.

The review meeting was held in the finance department conference room known as "the rock" because the window had a view of another FirstCorp building's stone façade. In some sort of twisted joke, the conference room down the hall was nicknamed "the hard place." Ironically, the project team offices were located between these two conference rooms.

It seems like ages have passed since the executive committee meeting placed the project on hold, Jenny thought to herself, mentally going over the list. Over the last week and a half, we've reviewed all of the project documents, cross-referenced them, interviewed the key participants, and developed our findings. Now it's time to present them to the executive committee before the meeting with Cindy. The goal here is not so much to present the findings, because as Bill said, the findings "are what they are," in the sense that they are a factual representation of the situation. The goal is to gain consensus among the players and determine the go-forward plan.

To give everybody a heads-up, Bill had e-mailed Brett, Mary, and Bobby the findings report ahead of time and was able to speak briefly with Brett and Bobby to get their feedback. He was unable to catch up with Mary, who was still knee-deep in HR issues.

"Has everyone had a chance to review the report?" Bill asked. Brett, Mary, and Bobby nodded in response. "OK then, let's walk through the assessment. First, as you know, Jenny and I spent a great deal of time reviewing where we are in the project. We reviewed and cross-referenced the critical project documentation from the start of the project and have spoken with each of you. From this assessment, we have gathered our findings, dividing them into the following sections: Project Management, Functional, Technical, and Change Management. Each section has a summary of the current state of the particular area with recommendations for improvements or areas of concern," Bill said.

"Let's start with Project Management. Overall, the project is showing a red status—meaning that the project team has missed critical milestones and that there are a number of show stopper issues with the software," Bill paused before going on. "On the positive side, we do have a good project management structure to track progress, issues, and risks. We just haven't been able to act because the executive committee feels like a decision can't be made without top management—Cindy—being involved."

"Are you sure you want to keep that last part about Cindy?" Mary asked. *"I don't think it would be wise to call her out."*

"Well, maybe we could change the wording or just bring that up in the course of discussion," said Bill, *"but, given the fact that it is such a major issue, don't you think it needs to be addressed?"*

"Ummm," Mary started.

"I do," Brett chimed in. *"I mean, a lot of this is her fault. I think we should call her out."*

"I don't think you want to go that far," Bobby interjected.

"We absolutely need to bring this up with Cindy," said Jenny. *"If we don't, we won't have the executive support to get what we need. If she wants things to get better, she has two choices: become more involved or delegate more authority."*

"Or kill the project," Mary said, cutting her off.

"Or kill the project," Bill agreed, *"but that decision is beyond us. Now, I don't want to put my head on the chopping block any more than you do, but we need to address this with her. I can leave it off the written report, but bring it up in discussion."*

"I would be more comfortable with that approach," Mary submitted.

"OK, then we will go with that," Bill concluded. "If there is nothing else on Project Management, let's move on to the Functional Section."

"On the financial side, the project team is on track with the exception of several critical issues with the software. Jenny is working with Lisa at BusinessWare and the software issues have been escalated to the highest level possible. We are expecting patches and fixes to be delivered no later than next Friday," said Bill.

"I am glad we had that conference call," Jenny chimed in. "Lisa has been super-responsive and I'm seeing progress."

"Good." Everybody agreed.

Bill continued. "As for the HR side, things are not as great. The team is two months behind for various reasons, but mainly because they were late to join the project team and their resources are spread too thin. Mary, do you agree with this assessment?"

"Yes," she replied, "but I would also like to add the discussion that we had with Parnew about converting to their system."

"I think that's a great idea," Bill said. "On the technical side, IT has stabilized the environment. At this point there are no serious issues."

"Well, that is not entirely true," Brett added. "We have to do something about the constant requests for security access, data refreshes, and more environments."

"What, you need more business requirements?" Tim said sarcastically.

"No," Brett replied. "I understand that there will be requests and some are legitimate and others are not. I need you and Jenny to do a better job of vetting these requests from the project team and then requesting a reasonable turnaround time for noncritical requests."

"I think we can do that," Jenny said.

"Good, that would make things a hundred times better," said Brett.

"If there is no further discussion of the technical issues, then let's talk Change Management," Bill continued. "As you may have noticed, I did not invite Janice to this meeting, because some of this discussion will involve her.

"From what Jenny and I can tell, we are missing the boat on change management and this cutover is going to have a significant impact on the end users. I know from my past company experience that in finance, the users are going to have to learn more about both accounting and the new system. They are no longer going to be able to enter smart codes for transactions to create the

accounting entries; they are going to have to learn and enter the accounting entries themselves."

"From talking with the HR VP at Parnew, the situation will be similar for HR staff," Mary added. "I have to say I am very concerned about this."

"This is one area where we need help, but I am not sure we have the people in-house to do it," Jenny said, and added, "Bill and I were thinking we could get a proposal from Bobby on what it would cost for CYA to take this over."

"I think we can do that," Bobby quickly replied. He always seemed to be more alert when new services were involved.

"OK," Bill asked, "does everybody agree with these findings?"

A unified "Yes."

"Great." Bill paused. "But before we move on to the recommendations, let's summarize the findings."

1. *The project status is red and there are a number of show stopper issues with the software.*

2. *With a few exceptions, the financials implementation is on track, but HR is behind and slipping.*

3. *The technical environment is stable, but better processes need to be put in place regarding requests from the project team.*

4. *The change management and training effort will be significant and we do not have the resources in-house to meet the project scope and timeline.*

"So here are my thoughts on recommendations," Bill said, approaching the white board.

1. *We need executive involvement, either in the form of Cindy or in her empowering the executive team to make the go-forward decisions.*

"I agree," Mary said, "just tread lightly with that one."

"Will do," Bill continued.

2. *We need to escalate the critical issues with BusinessWare. We already started this with our conference call the other day and, as Jenny mentioned, the vendor has been very responsive.*

"And, although this one is not as critical as the others," Bill stated, "let's just get it out of the way."

3. *Implement a prioritized vetting process for project team requests to IT.*

"Now for some tougher issues. What do you guys think we should do in the functional areas?" Bill asked.

"Well, it sounds like, for the most part, the financial project is on track," said Bobby.

"Agreed," Jenny replied.

"You know what I would like to see?" asked Mary. "At this point, we really should put HR on hold to conduct an assessment of the new company's HR system and determine if it is a viable solution."

"Plus, if we continue down the current path, we may not have the resources or ability to digest both a new HR and a new financial system at this time," Brett added.

"That's a good point," said Mary.

"Well, what about our consultants?" Tim asked.

"We would roll them off," Bill replied.

"You know," Bobby started, "you could use the cost savings on not continuing with HR for change management and training."

"Good idea, Bobby, but given all the money we are spending with you guys, we are expecting the go-live party to be at your lake house," Jenny said.

"I think we can do that," Bobby replied with a grin.

"OK, so that takes care of HR and Financials," said Bill. "But what should we do with Janice?"

"I have a thought," Brett added. "Janice was the project manager for our current HR system; she would be a good person to lead the assessment of the HR system conversion to Parnew's system. Mary, would you be comfortable with that?"

"Very comfortable," Mary replied.

"Good, then it's a win-win solution," Bill said. "So, in summary, our final recommendations are as follows."

4. *Continue with the Financials implementation and critical issue resolution.*

5. *Place the HR system on hold and conduct an assessment to determine if we should convert to the new company's systems.*

6. *Use the cost savings to have CYA Partners provide change management services.*

"Are each of you comfortable with the recommendations?" Bill asked.

Everybody nodded in agreement.

"Good, I will put together some slides for the meeting with Cindy and will send them to you before the meeting," said Bill. "Also, I appreciate your open-mindedness for this assessment as I know many of you

were skeptical to begin with. I know that these recommendations are high level and there is a lot of work for us to do, but I think they are reflective of the best path forward. You all have done a lot of good work and we are too close on finance to stop now. Freeing up some resources from the HR side to apply to change management will definitely help get us across the finish line. See you Friday."

The meeting with Cindy
Cindy's office was located on the twentieth-floor in the executive suite of the FirstCorp headquarters. The executive suite had great panoramic views of the city and was decorated with awards, marketing slogans, and framed articles about the company's successes, not the failures or train wrecks.

Jenny felt immediately that their fate would be determined in the next hour. Everybody was a little nervous, even Bobby and Charles. Both of them had had plenty of executive interaction, but they knew the situation was serious and that there was always the potential to lose business or profits. Even though they were senior executives with their firms, they, too reported to people who demanded results.

They were led to a waiting area and told that Cindy was wrapping up a conference call with Ted about the Parnew acquisition. They waited nervously in the waiting room, fidgeting and making small talk. After a half hour, Cindy emerged and asked them to get set up to present while she stopped by her office to grab a bottle of water.

Cindy Jackson was the COO of FirstCorp, a job she had earned by working her way up through the ranks. She had started out as an administrative assistant and quickly rose through management, tackling everyone and anything in her way. She had gained a reputation as a tough-nosed negotiator who made quick decisions. Everyone knew that if you were going to present to Cindy, you had to have your ducks in a row. The same held true for this project. It was initially spearheaded by Cindy, but after the Parnew acquisition, she was needed elsewhere. The problem was that she never really gave up the position of executive sponsor of the project that was now in jeopardy.

Cindy walked in with her portfolio and bottle of water. Despite the fact that it was four on a Friday afternoon, she appeared as crisp as ever and seemed in no hurry to go anywhere other than on to more meetings.

Great, Jenny thought. Hope no one has plans for dinner.

"So, have you had a chance to settle in here at FirstCorp yet, Bill?" Cindy asked, cracking a smile.

"Oh yeah, out of the frying pan and into the fire," Bill shot back.

"I guess you didn't expect this trial by fire on your first two weeks on the job," Cindy said.

"No, not exactly how I imagined things, but it is what it is," Bill said, as he handed out the presentation. "Let's get started, shall we?"

The final report was not more than a few pages long, but in order to get the major points across to Cindy, Bill and Jenny had condensed the report to a couple of slides.

Bill opened the meeting. "First off, Cindy thanks for giving us some of your time today. At your request, the team here, led by Jenny and me, has conducted an assessment of the current state of the project. As you know, the status of the project is not good. From our assessment, which consisted of a thorough review of all project documentation and interviews with all the key players, if the project was allowed to continue to progress in its current form, it would most likely fail. If you look at the first slide, you will see an outline of our process, the documentation we reviewed, and the people we interviewed."

"OK, sounds like a good process, Bill, so what are the results?" asked Cindy.

"Well, let's start with the good news," stated Bill. "The financial system implementation is on track, and, while we've had a few critical issues with the BusinessWare applications, Charles and his team have escalated the issues with their development people. We expect fixes to be delivered by next week."

"Well, that is good news, Charles," said Cindy. "We've spent a great deal of money with you and we expect that this project will mean as much to BusinessWare as it does to FirstCorp."

"It absolutely does, Cindy," responded Charles. "We've had a few miscommunications, but I can assure you that things are back on track. I'm getting daily updates from our team on the status of your issues. You have our full commitment."

"Good, we expect nothing less," Cindy responded. "OK, Bill, that's the good news—now what's the bad?"

"The HR implementation is behind for a number of reasons," Bill continued.

1. HR was late to the project and did not have time to fully define their requirements.

2. The project is taking place in the middle of open enrollment and the resources are spread too thin with the Parnew merger.

"Well, this is disappointing news, but I understand the situation. We just can't stop the HR implementation," Cindy responded. "Can it be fixed?"

"We aren't sure yet," Bill said. "Through our assessment, Mary brought up the idea of converting to Parnew's system or finishing the remediation of the legacy system. Either way, given the resource *requirements, we are not sure we can complete both the financial and HR implementations."*

"Bobby, what is your take on this?" Cindy asked. "I believe it was your firm who recommended that we do both. If we cancelled HR, we would expect some concessions from you."

"Well, we didn't anticipate the merger and we underestimated the impact of open enrollment on HR," replied Bobby. "I don't want to pre-empt Bill, but that will come later in the report."

"Good, so what is the team's recommendation?" asked Cindy.

"We need to stop the HR implementation and look at either moving onto Parnew's system or finishing the remediation and implementing the BusinessWare modules later. Either way, we need more time to study the options," declared Bill.

"What about the integration between timekeeping and project costing?" asked Cindy, "Wasn't that why we were doing this in the first place?"

Boy, she has a good memory, Jenny thought to herself. I guess you don't get to Cindy's level unless you are pretty sharp.

"We think we can handle that through an interface," Tim offered.

"Holy cow, where was that idea seven months ago before we headed down this path?" Cindy erupted. The room fell silent.

"Let's go ahead with the assessment findings and not worry about how we got here," Bill said quietly, breaking the tension. "We can table that discussion for the contract review with CYA."

"OK, so finance is on track, HR is off track. What else?" Cindy asked.

"Two things," said Bill. "First, in order for finance to be successful, we need more of a focus on change management. We have asked Bobby to develop a scope of work proposal to provide that service. We can divert some of the funds from the HR implementation and training to change management—and given the situation with the HR project, I am sure Bobby will give us a good deal on the services."

"All right, what is the second thing?" Cindy asked.

"Well, we know that you are tied up with the Parnew acquisition, but we need to make sure we have more of your time for decision making or that you empower the executive team to make decisions. Some of these unresolved issues have been floating around for a while because there is confusion about who can make decisions," Bill explained quietly.

"I assumed that you guys were making most of the decisions, but items of this magnitude need to be brought to my attention. Given my schedule, I'm unable to make the current executive committee meetings, but I need to be kept abreast of what is going on," Cindy stated. "From here on out, let's set a fifteen-minute, bi-weekly briefing, in person or conference call, with all of us—Bill, Brett, Mary, Bobby, Charles, and Jenny—preferably before the day gets started, to make sure you have my attention or if there are decisions that I need to be involved in."

"Sounds good," Bill replied.

"Do you think we can make the go-live date for Financials?" Cindy asked.

"Probably," Bill replied. "We may need to do some more analysis to be sure."

"We cannot keep changing the date," Cindy stated flatly. "If we need to change it again, we better make sure that this is the last time we do it."

"Got it," everybody replied.

"Bobby, when can you get us that proposal?" Cindy inquired pointedly.

"I should have it early next week," Bobby responded.

"Let's do this," Bill summarized. "We have a couple action items: One, we need to do some more research

on the go-live date for Financials; two, get a timeline for the HR assessment; and three, get a proposal from Bobby for additional change management services. In addition, we'll go back and do our due diligence in these areas and then we will regroup with you at the same time next Friday. Are you comfortable with that, Cindy?"

"Yes," she nodded her head, punching the meeting date and time into her Smartphone.

"Is everyone else comfortable with this approach?" asked Bill.

"I'm not sure that is enough time, "Mary and Tim both protested, but stopped once they got a glare from Cindy.

"Ah, sure, I think we can get it done," Bobby broke in.

"One more thing," Cindy said. "I appreciate the work you guys did on this assessment and I am glad we stepped back for a minute to look at the situation. But make no mistake; I'm not happy with all that has happened surrounding the project, so let's keep our eyes on the ball moving forward. Understood?"

Everyone nodded, as if they had just been scolded by the teacher.

"All right then, I will see you next week," Cindy said. "I need to give Ted an update. Bobby, you may want to take your family out to dinner and a movie tonight, *otherwise Ted may be paying you one of those evening visits."*

"Got it, thanks for the heads-up," Bobby said, his eyes wide open as he headed for the door.[11]

Conclusion

Whether it is the story of Jenny, Bill, and the FirstCorp project team or projects from your organization, one thing is for sure: There is never a shortage of stories to tell. Whether you are reminiscing about the sales process, project team members, or steering committee meetings, the people and shared experiences are what make this such an interesting and often humorous business. However, few people find missing deadlines, unimplemented software, and wasting money funny.

Making significant changes to get an ongoing project back on track is tricky and relies more on the ability to change and influence human behavior than on the ability to update a project dashboard or conduct a fit-gap session. It also requires project leadership, not just project management. And, to further complicate things, the leadership may need to come from someone who is not in the position of authority, but who needs to convince the people in positions of authority that change is required for project success.

The Collaborative Intervention methodology provides a framework for stepping back from the situation and looking objectively at the project as a whole. Collaborative Intervention is a comprehensive methodology that identifies and assesses the gaps that lead to project failure and provides a framework and process for closing these gaps.

The Collaborative Intervention process works through three primary phases: identify, assess, and intervene.

> **Identify:** The first phase of the Collaborative Intervention process is to identify where the project is in its implementation lifecycle, so that you understand when to intervene. Once determined, you can know what to look for and what the likely issues may be.

> **Assess:** The second phase of the Collaborative Intervention process is to assess. The assessment is a top-to-bottom evaluation of what to look for during the project helping you align project expectations, resources, and scope with the goal of increasing the project's probability of success.

> **Intervene:** The final stage of the Collaborative Intervention process is to intervene. The Collaborative Intervention process outlines how to

intervene by presenting the findings of the assessment and working with the project team to develop an implementation plan to address the findings.

At the end of the day, Collaborative Intervention gives you the when, what, and how answers that you need to assure project success. It helps you to identify and resolve the strategic, tactical, and intangible issues before they become insurmountable.

Having Collaborative Intervention as part of a large-scale business system implementation helps you:

- Control/reduce project costs
- Ensure milestones are met
- Minimize surprises
- Provide objective analysis.

The incremental costs you will incur by having an additional resource periodically conduct project assessments will be far less than the cost of project delays caused by unrealized project gaps. Collaborative Intervention will provide the peace of mind that the project is on the right track and that the disastrous train wreck will never occur.

References

1. "Outsourcing: Industrialize your applications delivery to achieve high performance," Accenture, 2008 (http://www.mis-asia.com/__data/assets/pdf_file/0009/137367/AO-PoV---Industrialize-apps-delivery-for-HP.pdf).
2. "NZ Project Management Survey 2010," KPMG, 2010.
3. "Delivering large scale IT projects on time, on budget and on value," Michael Bloch, Sven Blumberg and Jurgen Laartz, *McKinsey Quarterly*, October 2012.
4. Wikipedia, http://en.wikipedia.org/wiki/Y2k.
5. "Profiles of World-Class Finance," The Hackett Group, 2003.
6. "Strategic Planning for the Enterprise Application Lifecycle," Future State Consulting, Inc., 2004.

COLLABORATIVE INTERVENTION

7. "Defining the Business Application Lifecycle,"
Gartner, Inc., September 2003.
8. Wikipedia (Sommerville, Ian (2007) [1982].
"4.1.1. The Waterfall Model". Software
engineering (8th ed.). Harlow: Addison Wesley.
pp. 66f. ISBN 0-321-31379-8.)
http://en.wikipedia.org/wiki/Waterfall_model#
Criticism.
9. Wikipedia
http://en.wikipedia.org/wiki/Project_Managem
ent_Professional.
10. Wikipedia http://en.wikipedia.org/wiki/IV%26V.
11. *No Wishing Required: The Business Case for
Project Assurance*, Rob Prinzo, copyright 2010.
12. *"The Impact of Business Requirements on the
Success of Technology Projects,"* from IAG
Consulting, 2009.

ABOUT THE AUTHOR

Rob Prinzo is the founder and CEO of The Prinzo Group and senior consultant with the firm. Rob works with organizations to develop and implement strategic plans, conducts workshops on the implementation of technology, and is the author of *No Wishing Required: The Business Case for Project Assurance* and *Project Soup: Recipes for Managing to Success.* For more information, please visit www.RobPrinzo.com.

26201726R00118

Made in the USA
Charleston, SC
27 January 2014